quick-fix
southern

Other Books by Rebecca Lang

Southern Entertaining for a New Generation

Mary Mac's Tea Room: Stories & Recipes from Atlanta's Classic Southern Kitchen

homemade
hospitality in
**30 minutes
or less**

quick-fix
southern

rebecca lang

**Andrews McMeel
Publishing, LLC**
Kansas City · Sydney · London

Andrews McMeel Publishing, LLC
an Andrews McMeel Universal company
1130 Walnut Street, Kansas City, Missouri 64106

www.andrewsmcmeel.com
www.rebeccalangcooks.com

11 12 13 14 15 RR2 10 9 8 7 6 5 4 3 2 1

ISBN: 978-1-4494-0110-8
Library of Congress Control Number: 2010930548

Photos by Sara Remington, pp. 10, 14; all other photos courtesy
iStockphoto.com

ATTENTION: SCHOOLS AND BUSINESSES
Andrews McMeel books are available at quantity discounts with bulk purchase
for educational, business, or sales promotional use. For information, please
e-mail the Andrews McMeel Publishing Special Sales Department:
specialsales@amuniversal.com

for mama
you are my quick-fix

contents

acknowledgments

I am incredibly indebted to my mother, Mandy Dopson, for all of her help while I was cooking, writing, and typing. I could not do what I do without her. My father and number one taste tester, William Dopson, worked harder than I can imagine for years, making sure I always had the things I needed and the education to get me where I wanted to go. As a parent myself, I now understand the sacrifices they both made so my sister and I could succeed.

My grandmothers gave me an appreciation of Southern food and the desire to always have a second helping. My cooking keeps me close to their memories. I so wish they both could turn these pages with me.

My sweet, sweet children, Camden and Adair, practiced patience far beyond their short years while I was busy making this book happen. Kevin, my husband, has given me a life that allows me to pursue my passion for food and a love in which to share it.

Natalie Schweers, my sister, is the only other person who shares my first memories of "cooking." We made some mean mud pies.

Carole Bidnick, my agent, is my biggest cheerleader, a good friend, and a wealth of knowledge. I am eternally grateful for her faith in me.

Jean Lucas has been much more than an editor. She's become my friend and a shining light along the way.

Everyone at Andrews McMeel has been incredibly welcoming and gracious. I am proud to be in the company of such talented professionals.

Nathalie Dupree gave me an opportunity years ago that paved the way for a career I adore. I owe her more than I can say.

Mary Moore and Virginia Willis have mentored me, given out countless pieces of advice, and nurtured my career. I thank them both a thousand times over.

Damon Lee Fowler, Jean Anderson, Nathalie Dupree, Gena Berry, Bubba Hopkins, and Laurie Moore offered their culinary, historical, and agricultural expertise.

Jeannette Dickey proofed my manuscript with the pencil of an English teacher and the knowledge of an experienced cook.

Sara Remington's flair behind the camera shows on the cover. I am grateful for her talent.

I am thankful for good friends and family members who turned their suppertimes into the favor of trying out a recipe: Meghan Garrard, Jennifer Jaax, Suzanne Kilgore, Suzanne Rutledge, Brooke Stortz, Mama, and my sister, Natalie Schweers. Meg Dure, Anne Segrest Freeze, Kitty Cobb, Peggy Galis, Meghan Garrard, and Eleanor Sams graciously answered all my questions.

I raise a proverbial glass to Jennie Schacht for all her help, her time, and the magic she works with words.

Linda Lang, my husband's mother, is a babysitter, errand runner, and everything else she can do to help when life and work get busy.

Our good family friend, Dink NeSmith, kept our supply of farm-fresh produce, sausage, and game birds stocked throughout all my recipe testing.

The Atlanta chapter of Les Dames d'Escoffier has been supportive in so many ways. I never cease to be inspired by this group of incredible women.

Dianne Jacob shared her expertise and wisdom to make my writing sing.

Thank you to Trish Parks for all your gracious help and sweet words.

I owe many friends a carpool pickup from school. I am so very grateful for their help when things were crazy in the kitchen. I am blessed with friends who have checked in with me, offered to help in any way, and shown how much they care.

Raising children isn't the only job that takes a village. A good book takes a small city.

introduction

It has often rested on the cooks to keep Southern culture alive by passing along the recipes for the food that is so much a part of the Southern identity. Passing down a love of cooking and a sense of place is pretty much a rite of passage for Southern grandparents. I learned what it is to have a love affair with food and an appreciation of the fare of the South from two incredible women, my grandmothers. We called them by untraditional names as long as they lived. Claudia Thomas was "Tom," and Sarah Dopson was "Sa."

Both of my grandmothers could run a kitchen like nobody's business. When Tom and Sa were cooking, everyone gathered round and waited to be fed. Friday night fish fries at Sa's house were filled with hot creamy grits, sweet tea in her favorite milk glass pitcher, and snacks of crispy tails of the fried fish as they were piled high on the serving platter.

Tom cooked such a big lunch every Sunday after church that we all napped for much of the afternoon. She served Coke in bottles and kept fried fatback on the back of the stove for treats. She made pimento cheese on the front porch and could whip up a batch of divinity without a recipe. With cooks like that only a few blocks away, I was destined to have a passion for home and the food that makes it mine.

There are practical explanations for many of the Southern dishes we eat today. Before the time of air-conditioning, frying was the cooking method of choice because it was fast and didn't heat up the kitchen like an oven. Pecans were eaten right out of the shell because they are abundant and native to the central South. Tomato plants love the heat and blazing sun of the Southern summers, so they have been on tables for generations. Biscuits were quick and easy and cooked up in a hurry. They were also portable and perfect for taking out to the fields.

Slaves who worked Southern farms and cooked in kitchens were the source of many traditional Southern foods. Yams, black-eyed peas, collards, and sorghum are just a few among that long list of foods and foodways that are now part of our heritage.

Southern food doesn't have to take hours in the kitchen. Most people think that the food of the South is a long process. I must admit that we do like to stand around and visit in the kitchen, but the time spent cooking can be short and sweet. With the same fresh food concept that my grandmothers lived by, I have mastered how to cook from scratch and still cook quickly. The ease of recipes like Soft Buttermilk Waffles, Slow Cooker Boiled Peanuts, and Fast Brunswick Stew defies all concepts that Southern food is a timely endeavor.

The recipes are easily readable, simple to make, and user-friendly even for beginners. Some traditional foods, like mustard greens that cooked on the stove for hours, often took longer than the time busy cooks have today. I've added flavor and shortened cooking times with techniques like slicing the greens into the ribbons and making casseroles and desserts in individual sizes. My Spicy Mustard Greens, Petite Chicken and Wild Rice Casseroles, and Upside-Down Chess Pies are just the beginning of a new Southern kitchen. Cooking tips are offered throughout the book to make even the most experienced cooks a little more efficient in the kitchen. Take a mini-class on Southern history by turning the pages and enjoying the tidbits of times gone by.

The chapters are arranged to fit right into the lives of cooks who have more things to do than there is time in the day. Choosing what to cook in the South, like everywhere else, often revolves around the time of day or happenings around town. Simply turn to the chapter to meet the perfect need, be it cocktail hour or taking a casserole to a new neighbor. From football games to dinner parties, it's all arranged for just the right occasion. Pick out a recipe, such as Divine Chicken and Dumplings, Soft Catfish Tacos, or Fresh Corn and Tomatoes for a weeknight dinner worthy of weekend praise.

Now, with a family of my own, my cooking has become faster, while still honoring my Southern roots. This rich combination of family, taste, history, and tradition brings me into the kitchen again and again.

quick-fix
southern

the basics of cooking quick in the south

Southern cooking doesn't have to take a long time to be comforting, satisfying, and filled with history and tradition. With a well-suited work area, a pantry stocked with ingredients you use most, and a few good tools, any kitchen can be a Southern kitchen. Even if your home is lacking the quintessential screen door and magnolia tree outside, you can cook Southern just like those of us raised below the "gnat-line."

Cooking is more than getting supper on the table or feeding a hungry crowd. It's the act of preparing something that will gratify and fill an empty spot for those you love. Quick cooking still provides that essential fulfillment for the cook. It just gets you to the end result a little faster.

Read on and learn some tips for making your life as a cook easier, the little things that make cooking faster and more satisfying. There's a simple reason that Southern food is prized for its comforting quality and rich cultural history: It's just so good.

about the recipes

The active time for all the recipes in this collection is 30 minutes or less. That means that the time spent actually prepping and actively working with the ingredients is a mere half hour at the most. There are make-ahead recipes that often make even the most hectic of times enjoyable. Some recipes, like casseroles and dishes made in the slow cooker, take some extra hands-off time. This hands-off time is listed at the top of these recipes.

At really busy times, these recipes are often more convenient than those that are ready to eat the moment they are done. With some time in the oven, or marinating in the fridge, or even cooking in the slow cooker all day, the cook has time to get more things done and even clean the kitchen before it's time to eat.

The recipes are all real, honest food. You will not find condensed soups or baking mix that are often found in other quick Southern recipes. Quick recipes can be made from scratch and still be fabulous.

the scoop on basic ingredients

Here are my standards that I go by in the kitchen. All of my recipes are tested to follow these guidelines.
- Milk is whole milk.
- Unless otherwise stated, all salt is iodized table salt.
- Chicken broth is boxed organic chicken broth.
- Buttermilk is whole buttermilk.
- Rotisserie chickens are about 2 pounds.

keys to quick cooking

keep a running grocery list

Being an organized grocery shopper really helps when pressed for time. Most people don't have time to go by the store several times a week. Keep a running grocery list at all times. As soon as I get back from a grocery trip, I start a new list. This way, I'm never out of an ingredient when I'm in the middle of a recipe. I also put things on the list when my supply dwindles so I don't ever run out.

grocery shop once

With your running grocery list, you never run out of staples. But to prevent other trips to the store, sit down and plan the week's meals. You can shop all at one time for the whole week. I plan grocery trips on days and times when the store is less crowded. Early in the morning and right after lunch are much less crazy in my local store.

a well-stocked pantry, fridge, and freezer

Keeping a pantry and fridge stocked with staples and a freezer that has last minute go-to items is a must. Keep perishables you use often in the freezer. I keep an entire shelf in the freezer full of nuts. I also keep odds and ends, like drumsticks and single pork tenderloins, to cook in a pinch.

I buy the smallest sizes of most packages, including spices, so nothing gets old in the cabinet. A spice cabinet is very personal and reflects the way you cook. I have always found the rule of throwing your spices out every six months incredibly wasteful and silly. Buy the very small containers of spices and write the month and year on the bottom of the container with a marker. Rub spices in between your fingers after several months to check the freshness. If it doesn't smell like what the bottle says it is, throw it out.

You know what works for your style of cooking, so stock the kitchen accordingly. If you came over and peeked at my staples on any given day, here is what you'd find:

pantry staples
- Almond butter (natural)
- Baking powder
- Baking soda
- Bread crumbs
- Boxed organic chicken broth
- Chocolate (semisweet, bittersweet, white)
- Cocoa powder (regular, Dutch process)
- Cornmeal
- Cornstarch
- Corn syrup
- Dried fruit
- Espresso powder
- Flour (all-purpose, self-rising)
- Garlic
- Green chiles
- Grits (stone-ground, quick)
- Honey
- Hot sauce
- Maple syrup
- Milk (evaporated, sweetened condensed)
- Mustard (Dijon, honey, coarse-grained)
- Nonstick cooking spray
- Oil (olive, vegetable)
- Olives
- Pasta, dried
- Peanut butter (natural)
- Preserves
- Rice
- Crisco shortening
- Soy sauce
- Sugar (brown, granulated, powdered, turbinado)
- Canned tomatoes (whole, diced, sauce)

- Vinegar (balsamic, cider, white, red wine, white balsamic, white wine, rice wine)
- Worcestershire sauce
- Yeast, active dry

refrigerated staples
- Bacon
- Unsalted butter
- Buttermilk
- Cheddar cheese
- Cream cheese
- Eggs, organic
- Goat cheese
- Heavy cream
- Lemons
- Mayonnaise
- Milk
- Nuts and seeds in the freezer (pecans, walnuts, pine nuts, almonds, sesame seeds)
- Parmigiano-Reggiano cheese
- Sour cream
- Yogurt

the well-equipped kitchen

Certain pieces of equipment and clever tools really save time in the kitchen. There are some things I now cannot function without. Cooking is certainly possible without items like these—it just takes a little longer.
- Food processor
- Cookie scoops in a few different sizes
- 2-ounce liquid measuring cup for measuring tablespoons of liquids
- Lemon squeezer
- Several sets of measuring spoons
- Several wet and dry measuring cups
- Microplane zester
- Can opener
- Slow cooker

- Several kitchen towels
- Silicone spatulas
- Good-quality dishwasher
- Oven thermometer

baking pan and dish sizes

dimension	capacity
7 by 11-inch	8 cups
9 by 13-inch	12 cups
8 by 8-inch	8 cups
9 by 9-inch	10 cups
4½ by 8½-inch	6 cups

about cast-iron cookware

Each cast-iron pan I own is older than I am. That's my general rule—my cast iron must have seen more years than I. Seasoned cast iron means that it has been oiled and heated many times, which gives the pan an almost nonstick surface. Older pans that have been used for years will be seasoned. New pans come with directions for seasoning.

Because they are made of iron, the pans will rust. To keep them in the best condition, these pans shouldn't be cleaned like other cookware. Cleaning after cooking can be done with a little water and a stiff brush. Heat the cleaned pan on top of the stove to thoroughly dry all the water and use a kitchen towel to rub on a light coating of oil. If my pan isn't particularly dirty, I simply rub with a hefty dose of kosher salt and wipe it clean.

If a pan has rusted, it will need to be reseasoned. Only now should you use soapy water and steel wool to remove the rust and clean the pan. Dry and lightly coat with oil on the inside and outside of the pan. "Cook" the pan in the oven at 400°F for about an hour.

clean as you go

I never cleaned as I cooked until I worked for Nathalie Dupree. After seeing me piling the sink high with dirty dishes on the first day, she said I would learn shortly how important it is to clean as you go. Boy, was she was right.

If you're really cooking, you have to be seriously cleaning. I only begin a recipe when my dishwasher and sink are empty. That way, I can load and wash as I go. It's never fun to wash dishes, but it's a lot less painful to do a little at a time instead of all of them after eating (when you're full and happy).

basic recipes

Making some easy Southern standbys, like self-rising flour and buttermilk, is much faster than making a trip to the store. Keep a batch of homemade barbecue sauce in the fridge for basting impromptu grilled chicken or saucing up a batch of barbecue. With the jump start from these basic recipes, any cook is well on the way to real Southern cooking.

basic recipes

southern all-purpose flour

makes 1 cup southern all-purpose flour

Southern flour, such as White Lily and Martha White, has less protein than national brands. This is because Southern flour is made from winter wheat, which is softer than summer wheat. Biscuits benefit especially from lower-protein Southern flour. Throughout the book, I call for Southern flour only in the recipes where it is essential. My grandmothers were religious about baking with White Lily, and I still use it today.

Look online (see Sources) for your own bag of Southern flour, or follow the recipe below to mix up a batch of flour that cooks very much like what Southerners can find in any grocery store.

Store the flour in an airtight container. Check the expiration dates on both the cake flour and all-purpose flour. Use the earlier date as your expiration date on your new batch of Southern flour.

½ cup cake flour
½ cup national brand all-purpose flour

Stir the cake flour and all-purpose flour together.

southern self-rising flour

makes 1 cup southern self-rising flour

National brands also make self-rising flour, but, like all-purpose flour, it is higher in protein than the Southern versions. Especially popular for making biscuits, self-rising flour has baking powder and salt mixed in.

Make sure to read the expiration date on the baking powder can. It makes a big difference. Write this date down to remember when your batch of self-rising flour should be replaced. Store the flour in an airtight container to keep it fresh.

1 cup Southern All-Purpose Flour (above)
1½ teaspoons baking powder
½ teaspoon salt

Stir the all-purpose flour, baking powder, and salt together.

toasting nuts

Toasting nuts brings out the natural oils and intensifies the flavor. The toasted nuts can be used right away or frozen for up to a year for later use. I toast large batches and keep them in the freezer for quick use. I like to toast nuts on top of the stove because it's easier and saves the energy of heating up the oven. The cooking times will vary based on the type of nut. Pine nuts will toast for about a minute, while walnuts and pecans take 3 to 4 minutes. Watch the nuts carefully because all types will burn quickly. Once a nut is burned, you can't go back.

Place the raw nuts on a large dry frying pan over low heat. The nuts should fit in a single layer. Use a spoon or spatula to move them around constantly. You can also shake the pan to keep the nuts moving.

Toast until they are light to medium brown, 1 to 4 minutes, depending on the type of nut. Remove the nuts from the pan immediately.

buttermilk

makes 1 cup buttermilk

Buttermilk is essential to so much of Southern cooking. When butter was still churned at home, buttermilk was the liquid left over after the butter was made. The romance of making buttermilk is all in the past. It's now created simply by adding bacteria to milk. If buttermilk, or even whole buttermilk, is hard to find in the grocery store, it's easy to make your own.

1 cup whole milk
1 tablespoon white vinegar

Stir the milk and vinegar together and allow to sit for 10 minutes. The milk will thicken slightly.

tangy barbecue sauce

makes 4½ cups

Mama always made her tangy barbecue sauce to go with my dad's ribs or chopped barbecue for family get-togethers on the back porch. I'll never forget the CorningWare saucepan she used with the removable handle. It's a miracle that pot wasn't dyed pink after years of holding the red, bubbling sauce.

¼ cup butter
1 cup finely diced Vidalia onion
2 cloves garlic, minced
3 cups ketchup

1 cup apple cider vinegar
¼ cup Worcestershire sauce
½ cup freshly squeezed lemon juice
½ cup packed light brown sugar

Heat the butter in a stockpot over medium-low heat. Add the onion and garlic and cook until softened, about 4 minutes. Stir in the ketchup, vinegar, Worcestershire sauce, lemon juice, and brown sugar. Bring to a simmer, stirring often. Cook for 10 minutes.

Keep the sauce in the fridge for up to 3 weeks.

sugar syrup

makes 3½ cups

I like to keep a jar of sugar syrup around for making sweet tea before lunch. It's often called for in recipes for cocktails and other beverages. Make as much as you need. It can be easily halved or doubled.

3 cups water
1 cup sugar

Combine the water and sugar in a medium saucepan over medium heat. Stir until the sugar dissolves, about 3 minutes. Remove the saucepan from the heat and cool for at least 10 minutes.

Store in the fridge for up to 1 week.

rise
and
shine

Sunrise in the rural South is an event everyone should experience at least once. There are no mosquitoes out that early, the gnats are still sleeping, and the birds are all you hear. The way the Spanish moss filters the new sunlight like an old porch screen is almost mesmerizing. Add a good cup of coffee and it's truly a magical time of day.

I learned what breakfast is all about from my dad. Each and every weekday morning started with one of his big hot breakfasts. He made sure that grits, bacon, and eggs were on my plate before I left for school. If I wasn't paying attention in class, it wasn't for lack of fuel. I'm sure it didn't hurt either to start the day together at the family table. Even now, I rarely eat cereal and I like the first meal of the day to be something enticing, not something out of a box or wrapper. A Sweet Potato Biscuit or a big bowl of Three-Cheese Grits gets me going each and every time. For the busiest mornings, I make Eggs in a Basket for a savory quiet moment.

I'd rather eat breakfast than all the other meals of the day combined. My husband, Kevin, and I got married in the morning simply so we could celebrate at the reception over a really huge breakfast. A big white dress, omelets, bacon, and cake—it doesn't get much better than that.

three-cheese grits

serves 6

Most non-Southerners who say they don't like grits have had poorly cooked grits. There's nothing worse than a grit that isn't done. The package cooking times on the quick grits are never enough. If the grits are crunchy, they aren't ready. The combination of Cheddar, cream cheese, and Monterey Jack creates a heavenly creaminess in every spoonful.

4 cups water
1 cup quick grits
2 ounces sharp Cheddar cheese

2 ounces Monterey Jack cheese
1 (8-ounce) package cream cheese
½ teaspoon salt

Combine the water and grits in a stockpot. Cook over medium heat for 20 minutes, stirring every few minutes. Make sure to scrape the bottom of the pan with the spoon each time.

While the grits are cooking, grate the Cheddar and Monterey Jack cheeses. When the grits are done, stir in the cream cheese, grated cheeses, and salt. Stir until the cheeses are melted. Serve immediately.

cooking school

Grits are made from corn kernels that have been split, rolled, and sifted. The finest granules to pass through the sieve are grits. The larger pieces are cornmeal. Quick grits have been rolled again to make them smaller in order to cook faster. Instant grits, which should be illegal, are precooked and dried and give grits a bad name.

peach yogurt parfait

serves 1

Breakfast doesn't get much quicker and easier than a parfait made with fresh fruit. This peach version is also pretty enough to serve as a first course to a special-occasion morning meal.

1 peach
2 tablespoons orange juice

½ cup vanilla yogurt
¼ cup plus 2 tablespoons granola

Peel and chop the peach and toss with the orange juice in a small mixing bowl.

In a clear parfait glass or large juice glass, layer half of the peaches, half of the yogurt, and half of the granola. Repeat the layers.

soft buttermilk waffles

makes 8 belgian-sized waffles

Tom would make big batches of her waffles for us to keep in the freezer at our house. The soft, fluffy waffles would be stored for morning cravings or afternoon snacks. I still prefer my waffles soft like hers. When the steam stops coming out of the waffle maker, the waffles are ready.

The waffles can be frozen for up to 2 months by placing sheets of wax paper in between each one and sealing them in a resealable plastic freezer bag. Place the frozen waffles directly in the toaster for 2 to 3 minutes, or until toasted and lightly browned.

¼ cup unsalted butter
2 tablespoons Crisco shortening
1¾ cups all-purpose flour
¾ teaspoon baking soda
1 teaspoon salt

⅓ cup sugar
1 large egg
1 cup milk
¾ cup buttermilk

Preheat a Belgian waffle maker according to the manufacturer's directions.

Combine the butter and shortening in a microwave-safe measuring cup. Melt them in the microwave, about 45 seconds.

Combine the flour, baking soda, salt, and sugar in a large mixing bowl.

Whisk the egg, milk, and buttermilk together in a medium mixing bowl and stir into the dry ingredients. Slowly pour the melted butter and shortening into the batter.

Lightly spray the heated waffle maker with nonstick cooking spray. Pour half (about 2 cups) of the batter in the waffle maker. Cook according to the manufacturer's instructions. Repeat with the remaining 2 cups of batter.

way back when

Crisco's popularity grew when a lard shortage occurred during World War I. Some Southerners still use lard (myself included) for some recipes, but vegetable shortening is much more common. Crisco is available in sticks that are much easier to measure.

baby vidalia frittata

serves 6

In the early spring, when the green tops of the onions are rising out of the sandy soil of South Georgia, there's a short window of time when you can buy baby Vidalias. Of course, most of the onions are left in the soil to be sold as "grown-ups." Once I see the baby onions in the stores, I use them in every recipe I can. The babies are similar in size to leeks. The time is short and the onions are tender and delightful. Use 1¼ cups sliced green onions if you can't find the little bitty Vidalias.

2 tablespoons olive oil
4 baby Vidalia onions, thinly sliced (white and green parts)
8 large eggs, beaten

¼ teaspoon salt
¼ teaspoon freshly ground black pepper
1 cup preshredded sharp Cheddar cheese
Fresh flat-leaf parsley, chopped

Move the oven rack to a position about 5 inches from the broiler. Preheat the broiler.

Heat the olive oil in an ovenproof, nonstick 10-inch skillet over medium heat. Add the sliced onions and cook, stirring often, for 6 minutes, or until soft. Arrange the onions evenly over the bottom of the skillet.

Combine the eggs, salt, and pepper in a medium bowl. Pour over the onions. Cook, uncovered, over low heat for 9 minutes. The center of the frittata will still be wet.

Sprinkle the cheese over the top of the frittata and broil until the cheese is melted and the eggs are cooked, about 1 minute. Sprinkle with the parsley before serving.

plantation scrambled eggs

serves 8

My great-aunt, Lillie Malcolm, made the best scrambled eggs I ever had. I can still see them piled gloriously high on her Franciscan Desert Rose platter she loved so much. I never got the recipe from her, but later stumbled on how to make eggs very much like she did. The key is adding half-and-half or cream and never letting the eggs stay still in the pan.

12 large eggs
½ cup half-and-half
½ teaspoon salt

¼ teaspoon freshly ground black pepper
Dash of hot sauce
1 tablespoon unsalted butter

Whisk the eggs, half-and-half, salt, pepper, and hot sauce in a large mixing bowl until thoroughly combined.

Melt the butter over medium-low heat in a large nonstick skillet.

Slowly pour the egg mixture into the hot skillet. Use a silicone spatula to push the eggs around the pan. Cook, using the spatula to move the eggs constantly, for 8 minutes, or until fluffy and just beginning to set. Serve immediately.

cooking school

Cracking eggs on a flat surface, like a countertop, yields a straighter break than cracking them on the side of a bowl. The straighter the break, the less likely bits of unruly shell will fall in the bowl.

slow-cooking stone-ground grits

serves 4

slow-cooking time: 6 hours

Stone-ground grits are ground in a stone mill and are much larger than quick- cooking grits. They also have an abundance of flavor compared to the faster-cooking versions. Most Southerners will put them on the stove and cook them for hours, sometimes even all day, while popping in and out of the kitchen to stir. Cooking them in the slow cooker requires no stirring at all. Let them cook all night and wake up to rich, creamy grits.

1 cup stone-ground grits
3½ cups water, plus additional for rinsing
   the grits

1 cup milk
2 tablespoons unsalted butter
2 teaspoons salt

Lightly spray a 6-quart slow cooker with nonstick cooking spray.

Place the grits in a medium mixing bowl and cover with water to rinse any debris. Stir gently and skim off any debris that floats to the top. Drain the grits and discard the water.

Add the grits, 3½ cups of water, the milk, butter, and salt to the slow cooker. Turn the slow cooker to the low setting, replace the lid, and allow to cook for 6 hours. Stir the grits well before serving.

eggs in a basket

serves 4

I am not one to eat a bowl of cereal for breakfast. If I'm in a hurry and need a real breakfast to last me until lunch, this is what I make. It's super-fast, crispy, buttery, and unbelievably satisfying. I like to leave the yolk a little runny and use the bread to mop around the plate.

2 tablespoons butter, divided
4 slices bread (¾ inch thick)
4 large eggs

Melt 1 tablespoon of the butter in a large nonstick skillet over medium heat. Cut a hole in the center of each slice of bread with a 3-inch round cutter.

Place 2 slices of bread and 2 circle cutouts in the skillet. Crack an egg into each hole. Cook for 4 minutes, or until browned. Flip and cook for 1 to 2 minutes more.

Repeat with the remaining tablespoon of butter, 2 slices of bread, 2 circle cutouts, and 2 eggs.

sweet potato biscuits

makes 13 to 15 biscuits

I like to save any leftover baked sweet potatoes I have for biscuits the next day. But you have to have a baked sweet potato. On most days, you won't have a baked potato and there are no canned, unsweetened sweet potatoes at the grocery store. So, stroll on over to the baby food aisle and pick up some sweet potatoes, ready and perfect for the job.

1/2 cup buttermilk
2 (6-ounce) jars sweet potato baby food
4 cups Southern All-Purpose Flour, plus
  more for the counter and your hands
  (page 7)

2 tablespoons baking powder
1 teaspoon salt
1 cup cold unsalted butter, cut into pieces

Preheat the oven to 425°F. Line a rimmed baking sheet with parchment paper or a silicone baking mat.

Stir together the buttermilk and baby food in a small bowl and set aside.

Combine the flour, baking powder, salt, and butter in the bowl of a food processor fitted with the metal blade. Pulse 7 times or until the butter is cut into very small pieces.

Add the buttermilk mixture and process until the dough comes together, about 15 seconds.

Sprinkle some flour on the countertop. Turn the dough out onto the floured counter. Flour your hands well and pat the dough to about ¾ inch thick.

Cut the biscuits with a floured 3-inch round cutter. Flour the cutter again before cutting each biscuit. Place the biscuits, about 1 inch apart, on the prepared baking sheet.

Bake for 16 to 18 minutes, or until slightly browned.

cooking school
. . . .
Twisting the cutter as you cut a biscuit can produce lopsided biscuits. Cut straight down as you slice through the dough.

wild mushroom quiche

serves 4

Thanks to the warm weather and "cut it with a knife" humidity, shiitake mushrooms grow very well in the South and are pretty easy to find from local farmers. I serve this flavorful pie at just about every time of day, not just in the morning. It's great for a luncheon or light supper.

2 tablespoons unsalted butter
¾ cup finely chopped Vidalia onion
7 ounces shiitake mushrooms, stems removed and caps finely chopped
½ teaspoon salt
¼ teaspoon freshly ground black pepper

1 (9-inch) frozen ready-to-fill piecrust in pan
½ teaspoon fresh thyme, chopped
2 large eggs
⅓ cup heavy cream

Preheat the oven to 425°F. Place a rimmed baking sheet in the oven as it preheats.

Melt the butter in a large skillet over medium heat. Add the onion and cook, stirring often, for 2 minutes. Add the mushrooms, salt, and pepper and cook 4 minutes, stirring often. Arrange the mushrooms and onion in the crust, covering the bottom of the crust completely. Sprinkle the thyme over the mushrooms.

Combine the eggs and cream in a small mixing bowl and slowly pour over the mushrooms and thyme. Place the quiche on the preheated rimmed baking sheet.

Bake for 15 minutes, or until set.

drop biscuits

makes 8 to 10 biscuits

I think of biscuits that are rolled and cut as being more dressed up than ones that are just dropped onto the baking sheet. Because they aren't rolled and cut, drop biscuits are a little faster to make. Wetter dough makes moister biscuits, so don't be alarmed at the gooey dough.

1¾ cups Southern Self-Rising Flour, plus
   more for hands (page 7)
1 tablespoon sugar

⅓ cup Crisco shortening
⅛ teaspoon salt
1 cup buttermilk

Preheat the oven to 450°F.

Combine the flour, sugar, shortening, and salt in the bowl of a food processor fitted with the metal blade. Pulse 5 times. Transfer the flour mixture to a medium mixing bowl.

Stir the buttermilk into the flour. Stir just until the buttermilk is incorporated and all the flour is moistened.

Generously flour your hands. Using four fingers, scoop out dough about the size of a kiwi. Toss the dough back and fourth in your hands about 4 times (like the game "hot potato").

Drop the dough onto an ungreased light-colored baking sheet. Flour your hands again and repeat with the remaining dough, leaving about 2 inches in between each biscuit on the baking sheet. Flour your hands again before shaping each biscuit.

Bake for 14 to 17 minutes, or until lightly browned.

cooking school

There are several different kinds of biscuits that Southerners claim as their own. Angel biscuits, or bride's biscuits, are made with yeast and leaveners and are very light and airy tasting. Cathead biscuits got their name thanks to their large size (about the size of a cat's head); they look a little rough on the outside while still being fluffy on the inside. The most labor intensive is beaten biscuits. They are folded and "beaten" over and over to make a very tender, rich-tasting bread. In the late 1800s, there was actually a machine invented to save housewives the extreme work of beating the biscuit dough. Beaten biscuit tables, topped with marble or stone, are now quite a find in antique markets.

tupelo orange smoothie

serves 1

With a quick whir in the blender, a healthy glass of sunshine is ready in a flash. Because Greek-style yogurt has more protein than regular yogurt, that full feeling lasts throughout the morning.

1 cup Greek-style vanilla yogurt
1 banana, cut into large pieces
⅓ cup freshly squeezed orange juice
1 tablespoon tupelo honey

Combine the yogurt, banana, juice, and honey in the bowl of a blender or food processor. Blend until smooth. Serve with a straw.

cooking school

Tupelo honey is like Southern liquid gold. Tupelo trees grow in swampy areas in the South. The prized honey has a longer shelf life because it takes longer to crystallize than other varieties. The flavor tends to be incredibly sweet and almost buttery.

lemony figs with lavender

serves 8

I once was the proud owner of one of the largest Brown Turkey fig trees I've ever seen. I actually saw the tree from the backseat of the realtor's car as we pulled into the driveway. I announced that this was "the" house before even walking inside. When we moved away, I checked the price on moving my tree to go with us. It was no surprise that it was much cheaper to "beg and borrow" figs from our new neighbors. Brown Turkey figs are common in the South. Any other variety will work just as well.

1 pound Brown Turkey figs (about 18 figs)
4 cups reduced-fat vanilla yogurt
⅓ cup honey
1 tablespoon finely chopped fresh lavender

1 teaspoon lemon zest
Lemon slices, for garnish
Lavender sprigs and blossoms,
   for garnish

Remove the stems from the figs and cut each fig into 4 pieces.

Divide the yogurt among 8 serving bowls. Top each bowl of yogurt with about 3 figs (12 pieces) and 2 teaspoons of honey. Sprinkle with lavender and lemon zest.

Garnish with lemon slices, lavender sprigs, and blossoms.

sipping on the screened porch

Spiked Lemonade   29

Lime Mint Julep   30

Magnolia Mimosas   31

Classic Sweet Tea   33
 (with Mint Variation)

Peach Daiquiris   34

Key Lime Martini   34

Watermelon Margaritas   35

Blackberry Bubbly   36

Strawberry Kiss   36

Herbed Bloody Mary   37

Screened porches have long been the setting for the ever-popular Southern cocktail hour. From the times when mothers and fathers waited on news of the war to nowadays when families settle in after soccer practice, porches are one of the most important places in the house. No matter the drink of choice, bourbon or champagne, no porches are as hospitable as the ones in the South.

Sitting down in a big rocking chair and sipping a drink is a refreshing ritual to be enjoyed alone or with guests. Welcoming visitors with a glass of something special is the ideal way to pique their taste buds and put them at ease. Even a Yankee can relax and take in the breeze with a Lime Mint Julep or an icy Peach Daiquiri.

Classic Sweet Tea and Watermelon Margaritas are an introduction to the South no one can resist. With glass in hand, perhaps a straw to the lips, the oaks seem a little taller, the breeze a little cooler, and the magnolias just a little greener.

spiked lemonade

makes 3½ cups

serves 4

Meyer lemons have become a popular choice of gardeners along the Southern coasts and throughout Florida. If you can't put your hands on Meyer lemons, use regular lemons. The lemonade will be more tart, so taste and add more sugar to suit your liking. Make a batch without the vodka so the kids can also enjoy.

1½ cups sugar
2½ cups freshly squeezed Meyer lemon juice
1 cup vodka
Ice

Fresh raspberries, for garnish
Fresh mint sprigs, for garnish

In a large pitcher combine the sugar, lemon juice, and vodka. Serve over ice with a straw in highball glasses. Add a few raspberries to the glass and garnish with a mint sprig.

cooking school

Meyer lemons are believed to be a blend of a lemon and an orange. Available from November to May, this special lemon has the sweet flavor of an orange with just a hint of the tartness of a regular lemon.

lime mint julep

serves 1

The Kentucky Derby is known for its mint juleps and ladies sporting magnificent hats. The julep is traditionally served in a short sterling silver cup. Because the condensation on the cup should not be touched, Southerners traditionally drink their juleps with their hands touching only the rim and bottom of the cup.

Most people don't own sterling cups, so choose a rocks glass instead. If you're not a fan of bourbon, add what works for you. Never stress over liquor.

2 tablespoons bourbon
¼ cup freshly squeezed lime juice
2 tablespoons clear crème de menthe

¼ cup sparkling water
Ice
Fresh mint sprig

Whisk or shake together the bourbon, lime juice, crème de menthe, and sparkling water. Serve over ice with a mint sprig.

cooking school

Crème de menthe comes in both clear and green. Unless a drink needs to be turned a bright green, choose the clear.

magnolia mimosas

makes about 10 cups

serves 8

Known as a favorite of Southern ladies, the mimosa has been enjoyed in the shade of magnolia trees and on porches for ages. Traditionally made with orange juice, the mimosa is a staple of breakfast and brunch gatherings. Adding a little peach liqueur simply gives some more bang for the buck.

6 cups orange juice
⅓ cup peach liqueur
1 (750-milliliter) bottle sparkling wine
   or champagne
Peach slices or orange rind strips, for
   garnish

Combine the orange juice and liqueur in a large pitcher or punch bowl. Just before serving, add the sparkling wine. Serve in champagne glasses and garnish with peach slices or strips of orange rind.

classic sweet tea

makes 8 cups

serves 6

There are very few things more Southern than sweet tea. Some like it sweeter than others, so play with the sugar to make it perfect for you. When it came to making tea, Sa was heavy-handed with her sugar scoop. I remember its pouring from the spout so loaded with sugar it looked a bit like syrup.

5 cups water
2 family-sized iced tea bags
3½ cups Sugar Syrup (page 9)
Ice

Bring 5 cups of water to a boil in a large saucepan, about 10 minutes. Remove the saucepan from the heat and add the tea bags. Allow the tea to steep for 5 minutes. Remove the tea bags and discard them.

Pour the sugar syrup into a pitcher with at least a 1-quart capacity. Add the steeped tea and stir to combine. Pour over ice to enjoy. Serve on the same day.

mint sweet tea

Add 2½ cups torn fresh mint leaves to the sugar syrup when you take it off the heat. After cooling for 10 minutes, strain and discard the mint leaves. Continue with the recipe as directed.

peach daiquiris

serves 4 to 6

To keep the peach color bright and fresh, use light rum. If you have time, frost the glasses in the freezer for a few minutes.

6 medium peaches or 3 cups frozen
   peaches, thawed
½ cup peach nectar

4½ cups ice
½ to ¾ cup rum

Peel and coarsely chop the peaches and place them in a blender. Add about 2 tablespoons of nectar. Blend until the peaches are completely pureed.

Add the ice and blend until all of it is crushed. Add the remaining 6 tablespoons of nectar and the rum and blend to mix. Serve in large wineglasses.

key lime martini

serves 1

In most recipes, using imitation vanilla is practically a sin, but because it's clear, the martini retains its light, enchanting green color while still offering the flavors of a key lime pie. Use less sugar syrup for less sweet tooth and more pucker.

3 tablespoons vodka
2 tablespoons Rose's sweetened lime juice
3 tablespoons Sugar Syrup (page 9)

⅛ teaspoon imitation clear vanilla extract
Ice cubes
Fresh Key lime slices, for garnish

Combine the vodka, lime juice, sugar syrup, and vanilla extract in a cocktail shaker. Add about ½ cup of ice cubes. Shake 10 to 15 times. Strain and serve in a martini glass garnished with lime slices.

cooking school

The longer a drink is shaken, the more watered down it becomes. For a stronger drink, shake a few times. For a weaker version, shake a little longer.

watermelon margaritas

serves 4

As a child, I remember seeing pickup trucks in the summer so overloaded with watermelons that I thought any bump in the road could bring a green and red "landslide." I used to be so nervous if I was in the car behind the sky-high stack of melons!

To keep the drinks from getting watered down, wait until serving to pour the margaritas over ice.

4 cup chopped seedless watermelon
5 tablespoons freshly squeezed lime juice
2 tablespoons orange liqueur

¼ cup tequila
Ice
Lime slices, for garnish

Combine the watermelon, lime juice, orange liqueur, and tequila in a food processor fitted with the metal blade or in a blender. Process until liquefied. Serve the margaritas over ice. Garnish each glass with a slice of lime.

blackberry bubbly

serves 8

Almost any flavor sorbet works in this sweet fizzing sipper. As the sorbet melts, the purple color sinks into the champagne. Scoop balls of sorbet up to 2 days in advance. Arrange in a single layer in an airtight container and freeze until it's time to serve.

½ cup blackberry schnapps
1 (750-milliliter) bottle sparkling wine or
    champagne
Boysenberry sorbet

Pour 1 tablespoon of blackberry schnapps into the bottom of each of 8 champagne glasses. Top each with sparkling wine, leaving at least 1 inch at the top of the glass. Using a melon baller or a small scoop, drop one small ball of sorbet into each glass.

The sparkling wine will fizz with the sorbet.

strawberry kiss

serves 8 to 10

Picking strawberries from the farm is a pastime I wish every little girl could experience. Carrying a basket as it slowly fills with vine-ripened goodness is almost as difficult as waiting to get home to eat all the berries. Southern strawberries are at their sun-kissed peak in April and May. This drink combines the sweetness of summer berries with the fun of bubbles in a glass. The strawberry puree sits on top of the sparkling wine and resembles a big juicy red kiss.

1 pound fresh or frozen strawberries,
    thawed
1 (750-milliliter) bottle sparkling wine or
    champagne
1 lime, sliced, for garnish

Remove the stems from the strawberries and place the berries in a food processor fitted with a metal blade. Process until pureed. Pour the sparkling wine into champagne glasses, leaving about 1 inch at the top of each glass. Add 2 tablespoons of pureed strawberries to each glass. Garnish with a lime slice.

herbed bloody mary

serves 1

I bought my first muddler after discovering the joys of drinking mojitos. I like using it so much, I tend to muddle at the bar whenever I can.

If you like this morning pick-me-up with even more pickup, use a larger amount of hot sauce. The Bloody Mary originated in Paris but has found a place on menus all over the South. With pickled okra on top and fresh herbs throughout, the South comes through in each and every sip.

¼ cup freshly squeezed lemon juice
½ teaspoon chopped fresh chives
½ teaspoon chopped fresh basil
⅔ cup tomato juice
3 tablespoons vodka
½ to 1 teaspoon hot sauce

½ teaspoon prepared horseradish
½ teaspoon Worcestershire sauce
¾ cup ice for shaking, plus more for serving
1 pickled okra pod

Place a small wedge of the juiced lemon, chives, and basil in a cocktail shaker and muddle until the herbs are crushed. Add the tomato juice, vodka, lemon juice, hot sauce, horseradish, and Worcestershire sauce. Add ¾ cup of ice. Shake and strain over ice in a highball glass.

Cut a slice through the okra, cutting about ¾ way up toward the larger end. Place the okra on the rim of the glass before serving.

cooking school

A muddler is a tool that is used to crush drink ingredients so the flavors will be released. It looks like a mini meat mallet with a long handle. If you don't have one, you can also use the handle of a wooden spoon.

chapter 4

appetizers
and
snacks

The first magnolia blossom of the summer, the first catch of the day, the first hummingbird in May—all have a place etched in my memory. The first bite of a meal is no different. It sets the tone for every other course. That original taste is what's talked about and seems to roll out the comforting red carpet to guests and family alike.

Create a dazzling beginning with recipes that are easy to make and are stars on the plate. Benne Seed Shrimp and Pepper Jelly Tarts explode with Southern flavor and tradition.

I like to have appetizers ready to snack on while everyone is getting settled in and things are finishing up in the kitchen. Think out of the box when planning the first course. Deviled eggs aren't just for sides anymore; they are great for passing on a tray. Blue Cheese and Bacon Popcorn hits the spot with not too much and not too little to eat before time comes for the knife and fork.

Whether serving a nibble to whet the appetite or as a heartier first course, do as the Southerners do and serve something that won't be forgotten.

slow cooker boiled peanuts

makes 18 cups

slow-cooking time: 20 hours

It's not hard to spot boiled peanuts for sale along the roadside in the rural South. Handpainted signs tease drivers every few hundred feet until they reach the stand with an enormous pot full of soft and salty peanuts.

Peanuts right out of the ground are called green peanuts. They are the traditional choice for boiling, but they can be hard to find and are very perishable. Some grocery stores carry green peanuts during the late summer.

Raw peanuts have been dried after being pulled from the soil. They are much easier to find than the green ones. Choose the salt amount based on how salty you like your boiled peanuts. There's no dainty way to eat them—just open the shell and start slurping. The peanuts will keep in the fridge for a couple of weeks.

16 cups raw peanuts in the shell (about 2 pounds)
15 cups warm water

¾ to 1 cup salt
1 tablespoon vegetable oil

Rinse the peanuts in cold water. Discard the dirty water. Transfer the peanuts to a 6-quart slow cooker.

In a large mixing bowl, combine 15 cups of warm water, the salt, and oil. Pour over the peanuts. Cover the slow cooker with the lid and cook on high for 20 hours. If the slow cooker lid doesn't fit tightly, check about halfway through the cooking time. You may need to add more water. Drain the peanuts to serve.

way back when

After the boll weevil destroyed much of Southern cotton in the late 1800s, peanuts became the new cash crop. George Washington Carver developed many novel uses for the peanut.

jalapeño deviled eggs

makes 24

It's almost unheard of to have any leftover deviled eggs, no matter the occasion. They've been a popular Southern treat since the 1920s. By the mid-1900s, plates made just for these stuffed delicacies were common on bridal registries. If you'd rather have a sweeter egg without the heat of the jalapeños, use 3 tablespoons of sweet pickle relish instead.

12 large eggs
¾ cup mayonnaise
1 tablespoon Dijon mustard

1 tablespoon finely chopped pickled
    jalapeño peppers
¼ teaspoon salt

Cover the eggs with about 1 inch of cold water in a large saucepan. Bring the water to a boil over high heat. When the water boils, turn the heat off and let the eggs sit for 10 minutes. Submerge the eggs under cold water. Peel the eggs while holding them in running cold water. Slice the eggs in half lengthwise.

Remove the yolks from the eggs and place in a medium mixing bowl. Using a whisk, combine the yolks, mayonnaise, mustard, peppers, and salt.

Carefully spoon the yolk mixture back into the egg whites.

cooking school

Older eggs are better for boiling. Some of the white pulls away with the shell when peeling really fresh eggs. When boiled eggs are overcooked, a green ring forms around the edge of the yolk.

spring vegetables with lemon herb dip

serves 8

For a quick party pleaser, try this refreshing citrus dip paired with the highlights of emerging spring produce. It's even better the next day, so save some last-minute time and make it ahead. Clip off whatever herbs you have out in the garden. It's fine to use a different combination. You'll need about ½ cup of herbs.

1 (8-ounce) package cream cheese, at room
  temperature
½ cup sour cream
Zest of 1 lemon
3 tablespoons freshly squeezed lemon juice
1 tablespoon finely chopped sweet onion
1 teaspoon finely chopped fresh oregano
1 teaspoon finely chopped fresh thyme
1 tablespoon finely chopped fresh flat-leaf
  parsley

1 tablespoon finely chopped fresh cilantro
2 teaspoons finely chopped fresh sage
2 tablespoons finely chopped fresh chives
1 cucumber, thinly sliced, for serving
2 red bell peppers, sliced into strips, for
  serving
1 pound baby carrots, for serving

Using a hand mixer, mix together the cream cheese, sour cream, lemon zest and juice, sweet onion, oregano, thyme, parsley, cilantro, sage, and chives. Transfer the dip to a serving bowl.

Serve with the cucumber, peppers, and carrots.

cooking school

Cut a small nonstick rug pad into sections about 12 inches across. They are great for using all over the kitchen to keep things from slipping and sliding around. Try a piece under the mixing bowl when you use a hand mixer.

watermelon and feta on a stick

makes 24 (4-inch) skewers

The saltiness of feta pairs wonderfully with the sweet, juicy watermelon. These are really pretty when served standing upright. If 4-inch skewers are difficult to find, cut larger ones down with kitchen shears.

1 (8-ounce) block feta cheese
1 small seedless watermelon
Freshly ground black pepper

Cut the feta cheese into 24 cubes (about 1 x ¾ inch). Cut each cube in half. Cut the watermelon into 48 cubes (about 1 inch square). You should have about 4 cups of watermelon.

Using 4-inch bamboo skewers, thread the cubes starting with the feta and alternating with the watermelon. Each skewer will have 4 cubes. Sprinkle pepper over the skewered cubes.

cooking school

For the juiciest watermelon, choose one that's heavy for its size. To check for ripeness, turn it over and look for a yellow flattened side. This is the side that sat in the soil as it grew.

benne seed shrimp

serves 6

Coating shrimp with both white and black sesame seeds makes for a beautiful presentation. Look for sesame seeds in the Asian section of the grocery store. Those are usually cheaper than the ones on the spice aisle.

1 tablespoon vegetable oil
1 teaspoon sesame oil
1 pound medium shrimp (about 26 shrimp), peeled with the tails on
¼ cup white sesame seeds

2 tablespoons black sesame seeds
½ teaspoon salt
1 cup orange marmalade
¼ cup Creole mustard
1 green onion, thinly sliced

Preheat the oven to 400°F.

Combine the vegetable oil and sesame oil in a shallow bowl. Add the shrimp and toss to coat. Combine both the white and black sesame seeds on a plate. Dip one side of the shrimp in the seeds. Place the shrimp, seed side up, on a rimmed baking sheet. Sprinkle the shrimp with salt.

Bake for 8 minutes. The shrimp will be pink and curled.

Meanwhile, heat the orange marmalade in a small saucepan over low heat until it is liquid. Remove from the heat and add the mustard and green onion. Serve the shrimp with the orange sauce.

cooking school

Sesame seeds go rancid fairly quickly. To keep them fresh longer, store them in the freezer.

pepper jelly tarts

makes 30

Pepper jelly is often served over a block of cream cheese with crackers. I can't say that presentation looks outstanding, but it sure tastes good. This recipe is a way to dress up this classic combo. I have spent quite a few days canning my own pepper jelly. I take it to parties as hostess gifts and eat the rest myself.

4 ounces cream cheese
2 (1.9-ounce) packages mini phyllo shells
⅔ cup pepper jelly
2 tablespoons toasted pine nuts (page 8)

Preheat the oven to 350°F.

Place ½ teaspoon of cream cheese in each phyllo shell. Top each with 1 teaspoon of pepper jelly.

Bake the filled shells for 15 minutes. Top each shell with about 5 pine nuts before serving.

spiced pecans

makes 4 cups

On many a Christmas holiday I have delivered these nuts to our neighbors for little holiday gifts. I also serve them on the bar when we have parties. Pretty much any time of day or in any season, I can find a reason to gobble them up.

¼ cup unsalted butter, melted
½ teaspoon garlic powder
2 tablespoons Worcestershire sauce
¼ cup soy sauce

1 teaspoon cayenne pepper
1 teaspoon salt
½ teaspoon paprika
4 cups pecan halves

Preheat the oven to 325°F.

Combine the melted butter, garlic powder, Worcestershire sauce, soy sauce, cayenne pepper, salt, and paprika in a large mixing bowl. Add the pecans and toss well to coat.

Spread the pecans in a single layer on a rimmed baking sheet.

Bake for 20 minutes, stirring once. Drain and cool the pecans on several layers of paper towels. Store at room temperature for up to 5 days.

cooking school

Pecans often don't get enough credit for their nutritional value. They are high in vitamin E, magnesium, fiber, and other antioxidants.

baked brie with fig preserves and pecans

serves 8

I make my own fig preserves at the end of each summer. I love them so much that I am incredibly stingy and tend to keep most of the jars for us to enjoy all winter. I usually cut the figs in half so my preserves still have large, plump fig pieces. When shopping for a preserve, try to buy one with noticeable pieces of fruit.

1 (8-ounce) wheel Brie cheese
¼ cup fig preserves
1 teaspoon chopped fresh rosemary

8 pecan halves
Crackers or French bread, for serving

Preheat the oven to 350°F.

Trim the rind off the top of the Brie, leaving a ¼-inch border around the edge.

Combine the fig preserves and rosemary in a small mixing bowl. Spread over the top of the trimmed Brie.

Bake for 8 minutes. Arrange the pecans over the preserves and bake for an additional 5 minutes.

Serve immediately with crackers or French bread.

blue cheese and bacon popcorn

serves 4 to 6

Thanks to a popcorn craze, the childhood staple is now on menus at some of the best restaurants around the South. It's no longer just for movie theaters and birthday parties. Make it a snack in a flash by using microwave popcorn. Crispy bacon and good-quality blue cheese make it a grown-up's favorite nibble.

Unwrap the cheese and place it back in the fridge until the popcorn is done. The cheese grates best when it's cold.

1 (3.3-ounce) bag natural microwave popcorn
3 tablespoons butter, melted

2 ounces Maytag blue cheese
4 slices cooked bacon, finely chopped
2 teaspoons chopped fresh rosemary

Pop the popcorn according to the package directions, being careful not to burn it. Pour the popcorn into a large mixing bowl. Drizzle about half of the melted butter over the popcorn. Grate about half of the cheese over the popcorn. Sprinkle with half of the bacon and half of the rosemary. Toss the popcorn and repeat with the remaining melted butter, cheese, bacon, and rosemary. Serve immediately.

smoked trout spread

makes 2 cups

chilling time: 1 hour

This is one of my most popular recipes. I take it to parties and always get rave reviews. Woodsmoke Provisions, a Georgia company, smokes rainbow trout with pecan shells for divine flavor—it's easily found around the South. If you can't find the pecan smoked trout, ask at the seafood counter for what is available. Any smoked fish will work.

½ pound pecan smoked trout
1 (8-ounce) package cream cheese, at room
   temperature
⅓ cup sour cream
Zest and juice of 1 lemon

2 tablespoons chopped fresh dill
1 teaspoon Dijon mustard
¼ teaspoon hot sauce
Fresh dill, for garnish
Crackers, for serving

Peel the skin from each trout fillet and discard it. Finely chop the trout. Combine the trout, cream cheese, sour cream, lemon zest and juice, dill, mustard, and hot sauce in a medium mixing bowl. Cover and chill for 1 hour. Transfer to a serving bowl and garnish with the dill. Serve with crackers.

chapter 5

picnics
and
packables

For heading out to a picnic at the river or packing up the car to take in the leaves at their peak in the fall, edible portability is a must. Pack a bag of Appalachian Trail Mix for the crew and enjoy the most peaceful road trip ever. Each of the recipes in this chapter can be bagged, sealed in a jar, or stuffed in a cooler to meet the needs of hungry mouths on the go. Even if the trip is simply out to the backyard for a neighborhood picnic, the food must travel.

When the sun starts to go down and the hot summer air begins to cool, lay out a picnic blanket and fill it with good friends and great food. Classic Pimento Cheese and Quick Icebox Pickles are ideal for an al fresco supper. No matter the occasion, the food can still be the star, wherever you are.

Southerners have perfected packable meals over the years. In the days of large family farms and working your own land, portable food had a completely different purpose. I remember hearing Tom tell stories of my great-grandmother packing up biscuits and syrup for the family to eat while they were working out in the fields on the farm. They were wrapped in kitchen towels, so the package was also the napkin.

classic pimento cheese

makes 1¾ cups

Every self-respecting Southern cook has a pimento cheese recipe. From slathering it on a sandwich to serving it as a dip or a stuffing for celery, no Yankee can get far down South without falling in love with this signature combination of simple ingredients. The one rule to remember is to always grate your own cheese. Preshredded cheese simply will not do. This classic version is best served between two slices of soft white bread.

1 (10-ounce) block extra-sharp Cheddar cheese
½ cup mayonnaise

1 (2-ounce) jar diced pimentos, drained
2 tablespoons finely diced white onion
⅛ teaspoon Worcestershire sauce

Grate the Cheddar cheese using the large holes of a box grater. Combine the cheese, mayonnaise, pimentos, onion, and Worcestershire sauce in a medium mixing bowl. Store in the refrigerator in an airtight container for up to 1 week.

white pimento cheese

makes 4 cups

This version is insanely good as a dip for veggies. Made with several cheeses, it's a downtown version of a country staple.

1 (10-ounce) block sharp white Cheddar cheese

4 ounces extra-sharp Cheddar cheese

4 ounces block mozzarella cheese

1 (4-ounce) jar diced pimentos, drained

1 cup mayonnaise

½ cup finely chopped toasted pecans (page 8)

Grate the white Cheddar, Cheddar, and mozzarella cheeses using the large holes of a box grater. Combine the cheeses, pimentos, mayonnaise, and pecans in a large mixing bowl. Serve on crackers, in a sandwich, or with sliced vegetables. Store in the refrigerator in an airtight container for up to 1 week.

way back when

In her 1928 book, *Southern Cooking*, Mrs. Dull, an icon of Southern food, suggested serving pimento cheese with coffee as the last course at dinner.

chipotle pimento cheese

makes 1½ cups

Hot peppers are pretty common in pimento cheese recipes. I prefer the smokiness of chipotles and like a touch of adobo sauce for extra creaminess. Spread this hotter version on sturdy or hearty crackers and everyone will be asking for the recipe.

1 (10-ounce) extra-sharp Cheddar cheese
1 (2-ounce) jar diced pimentos, drained
⅓ cup mayonnaise
1 chipotle pepper packed in adobo sauce, diced

½ teaspoon adobo sauce
2 teaspoons finely chopped fresh flat-leaf parsley
¼ teaspoon salt

Grate the Cheddar cheese using the large holes of a box grater. Combine the cheese, pimentos, mayonnaise, chipotle pepper, adobo sauce, parsley, and salt in a medium mixing bowl. Serve with crackers. Store in the refrigerator in an airtight container for up to 1 week.

cooking school

A chipotle pepper is a smoked jalapeño pepper that is usually canned with adobo sauce. The sauce is just as smoky and spicy as the pepper. It's hard to use an entire can at once, so spread any leftover peppers on a small baking sheet and freeze. Transfer the frozen peppers to a resealable bag for later use.

tomato and black bean salsa

makes 8 cups

My kitchen is always filled with tomatoes during the season for this Southern delicacy. I put each and every one to good use. Use Roma tomatoes when other varieties aren't in season.

2 (15-ounce) cans black beans, rinsed and drained
4 cups diced tomato
1 medium red bell pepper, diced
1 medium red onion, diced
½ cup chopped fresh cilantro
⅓ cup freshly squeezed lime juice

¼ cup olive oil
3 cloves garlic, minced
½ teaspoon salt
½ teaspoon freshly ground black pepper
½ teaspoon ground cumin
Tortilla chips, for serving

Combine the beans, tomato, bell pepper, onion, cilantro, lime juice, olive oil, garlic, salt, pepper, and cumin in a large mixing bowl. Serve with tortilla chips.

To store, cover and place the salsa in the refrigerator for up to 1 week.

quick icebox pickles

makes 4 cups

chilling time: 2 hours

Icebox pickles got their name for a good reason. They have to be stored in the refrigerator. This recipe is much faster than others because the pickles aren't canned or processed.

2 cups white vinegar
1 cup sugar
2 dried bay leaves
1 teaspoon salt
1 teaspoon whole black peppercorns

1 (1-pound) hothouse cucumber (usually sold in shrink-wrap)
½ medium white onion, thinly sliced into quarter rounds (about 1 cup slices)

Bring the vinegar, sugar, bay leaves, salt, and peppercorns to a boil in a medium saucepan, about 5 minutes. Remove from the heat.

Meanwhile, cut the cucumber into ⅛-inch-thick slices. You should have about 3½ cups of cucumber slices.

Divide the cucumber and onion slices between 2 (16-ounce) jars. Carefully pour the vinegar mixture over the cucumbers and onions to fill the jars. Screw the lids on the jars and chill for 2 hours before serving.

Pickles will keep in the refrigerator for 1 week.

cooking school

Placing a wet paper towel under a cutting board will keep it from sliding around.

peach salsa

makes 2 cups

Combining sweet, juicy peaches with fresh lime and a little hot pepper gives the tried-and-true tomato salsa some real competition. This salsa is beautiful paired with blue corn tortilla chips, or try it on grilled fish and chicken. No peach trees in the neighborhood? Use a 20-ounce package of frozen peaches.

1½ pounds peaches
¼ cup finely chopped red onion
1 teaspoon lime zest
2 tablespoons freshly squeezed lime juice
1 tablespoon finely chopped jalapeño
   pepper

2 tablespoons chopped fresh cilantro
¼ teaspoon salt
Tortilla chips, for serving

Peel and chop the peaches. You should have about 2 cups of peaches. Combine the peaches, red onion, lime zest and juice, jalapeño, cilantro, and salt in a medium mixing bowl. Serve with tortilla chips.

marinated roasted peppers

makes 3 cups

marinating time: 1 hour

It's not uncommon for neighbors to deliver overflowing baskets of peppers and tomatoes when summer gardens are bursting with the year's best produce. Southerners are constantly finding new and fun ways to make yummy use of all the peppers. This is a much quicker version of the picnic staple I often make when I'm lucky enough to have a bumper crop. Marinating the peppers right in the jar makes it ideal for travel.

1 (24-ounce) jar roasted sweet red peppers
¼ cup balsamic vinegar
¼ cup olive oil
1 clove garlic, minced
¼ teaspoon salt

¼ teaspoon freshly ground black pepper
3 lemon slices, about ¼ inch thick
4 ounces goat cheese, softened
Fresh bread

Remove all the contents of the jar and set the jar aside. Drain the peppers and slice into ½-inch strips.

Whisk together the balsamic vinegar, olive oil, garlic, salt, and pepper in a 1-cup measuring cup.

Place one-third of the pepper strips in the reserved pepper jar and top with a lemon slice. Repeat the layers twice. Pour the balsamic vinegar mixture over the peppers in the jar. Use a knife to move the pepper strips around to help distribute the dressing throughout the jar.

Screw on the lid and marinate the peppers in the refrigerator for 1 hour.

Serve with goat cheese and fresh bread.

texas caviar

makes 8 cups

This "caviar" is so versatile, it's worth keeping a batch in the fridge. Try it on fried fish, as a salad, with chips, or as a side dish with sliced tomatoes. Helen Corbitt, the director of food service at Neiman Marcus in Dallas, turned this dip into a trendy item in the 1950s.

2 (15.8-ounce) cans black-eyed peas, rinsed and drained (3 cups)
2 (11-ounce) cans shoepeg corn, drained (2½ cups)
1 medium red bell pepper, diced
1 large Vidalia onion, diced

¾ cup apple cider vinegar
6 pepperoncini peppers, diced
¾ cup liquid from pepperoncini jar
¼ cup packed light brown sugar
Tortilla chips, for serving

Combine the peas, corn, bell pepper, onion, vinegar, pepperoncini peppers and their liquid, and brown sugar in a large mixing bowl. Serve with tortilla chips.

To store, cover and place the caviar in the refrigerator for up to 2 weeks.

cooking school

Microwave hardened brown sugar for a few seconds to soften it up.

honeyed tomatoes and ricotta

makes about 25

I serve these to my family as part of our picnic supper at a summer outdoor concert. I pack the tomatoes in one container, the ricotta in another, and carry the crostini in a resealable plastic bag. I even carry a fun little bottle of honey for drizzling. I let my crowd assemble their own and don't have a single morsel to bring back home.

1 pint grape tomatoes
1 tablespoon olive oil
1 teaspoon red wine vinegar
1 teaspoon honey, plus more for drizzling
¼ teaspoon freshly ground black pepper

1 (15-ounce) container whole milk ricotta cheese
½ teaspoon salt
1 tablespoon chopped fresh oregano
25 crostini

Preheat the oven to 425°F.

Cut the grape tomatoes in half lengthwise.

Combine the olive oil, vinegar, 1 teaspoon of honey, and pepper in a small mixing bowl. Add the tomatoes and toss. Transfer to a rimmed baking sheet. Make sure the tomatoes are in a single layer.

Bake for 12 minutes, or until the tomatoes are soft and the skins are wrinkled. Cool slightly.

Meanwhile, combine the ricotta cheese, salt, and oregano in a medium mixing bowl. Spread about 2 teaspoons of the ricotta mixture on each crostini. Top with 2 to 3 tomatoes per crostini. Drizzle with honey before serving.

cooking school

Honey likes to get stuck in the measuring spoon. Spray the measuring spoon with nonstick cooking spray before adding the honey and it will slip right out.

pickled wild shrimp

serves 8

chilling time: 8 hours

I first learned to love pickled shrimp while I was living in Charleston, South Carolina, during culinary school. I was fortunate enough to work for a caterer who knew low-country food and how to make it. Some serve the shrimp with toothpicks and others as a salad.

⅓ cup vegetable oil
½ cup white wine vinegar
¼ cup white balsamic vinegar
1 tablespoon green peppercorns, drained
2 dried bay leaves
½ teaspoon salt
⅛ teaspoon freshly ground black pepper
1 tablespoon sugar

Zest and juice of 1 lemon
1 tablespoon capers, drained
¼ teaspoon cayenne pepper
¾ teaspoon celery seed
2 pounds cooked peeled medium shrimp, tails on
1 medium Vidalia onion, thinly sliced

Combine the vegetable oil, white wine vinegar, white balsamic vinegar, green peppercorns, bay leaves, salt, pepper, sugar, lemon zest and juice, capers, cayenne pepper, and celery seed in a medium mixing bowl.

Place the shrimp and onion in a large resealable plastic bag. Pour the vegetable oil mixture over the shrimp. Seal the bag and chill for at least 8 hours.

Serve with a slotted spoon.

cooking school

Look for green peppercorns with the olives and pickles in the grocery store. They are packed in brine and bottled in small jars.

pickled okra and ham wheels

makes about 40

chilling time: 3 hours

Pickled okra and ham wheels have graced Southern party tables for years. They are often made with prepackaged flavored cream cheese and packaged ham. I like to freshen them up by mixing up my own cream cheese and using ham sliced fresh at the deli.

1 (8-ounce) package cream cheese, at room
   temperature
1 tablespoon chopped fresh chives
1 tablespoon chopped fresh flat-leaf parsley
3 tablespoons finely diced Vidalia onion

1 (16-ounce) jar pickled okra, drained
   (about 18 okra pods)
⅓ pound thinly sliced Virginia ham (about
   8 slices)

Combine the cream cheese, chives, parsley, and onion.

Trim both ends off each okra pod. On a large cutting board, lay out each slice of ham. Spread about 2 tablespoons of the cream cheese mixture on each slice of ham, leaving a border of about ¼ inch.

On the long side of each ham slice, lay the okra pods, end to end. Depending on the size of the ham slice, 2 to 3 okra pods will be needed. Roll the ham over the okra. Cover and chill the ham rolls for 3 hours.

Slice the rolls into 1-inch-thick slices and serve.

appalachian trail mix

makes 6 cups

The Appalachian Trail is a footpath that leads all the way from Georgia to Maine. Springer Mountain is just a short drive from our home and is at the southern tip of the trail. Hiking through the South is the best way to get a real look at the beauty of the land. For hiking or a simple stroll through the neighborhood, a snack of trail mix is an easy way to boost energy and get a quick protein punch.

1 (1-pound) jar roasted salted peanuts
¾ cup golden raisins
½ cup candy-coated chocolate pieces

¼ cup dark chocolate chips
½ cup peanut butter chips

Combine the peanuts, raisins, candy-coated chocolate pieces, chocolate chips, and peanut butter chips in a large mixing bowl. Store the trail mix in an airtight container for up to 2 weeks.

chewy granola bars

makes 16 bars

cooling time: 1 hour

Making a double batch of these bars is never a bad idea. Adults like them as much as children. Don't worry if the bars are very pliable when warm—they firm up as they cool.

3 cups oats and honey granola
1 cup crispy rice cereal
¾ cup sweetened dried cranberries
⅔ cup finely chopped toasted pecans
    (page 8)

½ cup light corn syrup
½ cup packed light brown sugar
1 tablespoon vanilla extract

Lightly grease a 9 by 13-inch pan with nonstick cooking spray.

Place the granola in a food processor fitted with the metal blade. Pulse 4 times.

Combine the granola, rice cereal, cranberries, and pecans in a large mixing bowl.

In a medium saucepan, bring the corn syrup and brown sugar to a boil, stirring constantly, over medium heat, about 4 minutes. Remove the saucepan from the heat and stir in the vanilla extract.

Working quickly, pour the corn syrup mixture over the granola. Stir to combine. Transfer the granola mixture to the prepared pan. Place a sheet of wax paper in between your hand and the granola and press into the pan.

Allow the bars to cool for about 1 hour. Turn the pan upside down on a cutting board to remove the uncut bars. Cut the rectangle into 16 bars. Store the granola bars between sheets of wax or parchment paper in an airtight container for up to 2 days.

salads, soups, and sandwiches

I learned the term "midday meal" from a man who was perhaps the greatest influence in my father's life. I like that old Southern term because it reminds me of a time when lunch was enjoyed around the table, just as supper is today. People came in from the fields, washed up, and sat down for the midday meal. My father's loyal friend was about as Southern as a man could get. He was a farmer, a naturalist, a gentleman, a postcard collector, an author, a tree farmer, a scholar, and a dozen other things. He could grow a bumper crop of peanuts, handle a shotgun with ease, and was a prolific writer of words in many forms. I am grateful to have had the privilege of cooking for him on a number of occasions.

When the sun reaches its highest point in the day, it's no time to skip the enjoyment of eating and race through the meal. I cherish the days when I have the time to step outside, pick a tomato, slice it while it's still warm from the sun, and share it at the table.

With these fast recipes, you can be done in the kitchen and have a few spare moments to savor. With dishes like Herbed Tomato Sandwiches, Sweet Onion Slaw, and Little Beet Salad, you'll be eating before you know it. My Fast Brunswick Stew is almost unbelievable and Bacon Vinaigrette with Salad Greens will turn anyone into a salad eater. Put on the apron and enjoy the best of both worlds—quick cooking and time at the table.

sweet onion slaw

serves 8

chilling time: 8 hours

Leave the cabbage out of this slaw and showcase South Georgia's finest crop. I was practically surrounded by sweet onions each summer thanks to growing up in Vidalia country. Like many Southerners, we always make the most of what grows close to home.

¾ cup sugar
1½ cups white vinegar
3 pounds Vidalia onions
¼ cup mayonnaise

2 tablespoons coarse-grained mustard
2 tablespoons chopped fresh flat-leaf
  parsley

Combine the sugar and vinegar in a large mixing bowl. Whisk until the sugar is dissolved.

Slice the onions in half and then slice thinly, creating half-moons. Add the onion slices to the vinegar mixture and toss well. Cover and refrigerate for 8 hours, stirring occasionally.

Drain the onions well. Add the mayonnaise, mustard, and parsley before serving.

cooking school

Vidalia onions are grown in an area surrounding Vidalia, Georgia. The sandy soil is low in sulfur and was accidentally found to produce sweet onions in the 1930s. Vidalias are best stored in a dry, dark place. Give the onions some space; they tend to go bad quicker if they are touching each other.

bacon vinaigrette with salad greens

serves 8

Marti Schimmel, a friend and caterer in Athens, makes an addictive sweet onion dressing. Thanks to her inspiration, I threw some bacon in my recipe and now have a dressing I could drink with a straw (if no one was watching).

6 slices bacon, chopped (about 6 ounces)
3 tablespoons honey
1 tablespoon Dijon mustard
¼ cup chopped Vidalia onion
3 tablespoons cider vinegar

⅛ teaspoon salt
Pinch of freshly ground black pepper
Vegetable oil (about ¼ cup)
2 (5-ounce) packages mixed salad greens

In a large skillet over medium heat, cook the bacon until it is crisp.

Meanwhile, combine the honey, mustard, onion, vinegar, salt, and pepper in the bowl of a food processor fitted with a metal blade. Pulse until the liquid is smooth.

Use a slotted spoon to transfer the bacon to a paper towel–lined plate. Reserve the drippings. When cooled slightly, pour the drippings into a 1-cup measuring cup.

Add enough vegetable oil to the bacon drippings to make ½ cup.

With the food processor running, slowing add the drippings and the oil in a steady stream.

Add 2 tablespoons of crisp bacon and pulse 3 times.

Drizzle the dressing over the salad greens. Serve the remaining bacon over the salad.

Store any remaining dressing in the fridge for up to 1 week.

cooking school

Never throw away bacon grease. It's as close to liquid cooking gold as you can get. Add it to the frying pan for sautéing vegetables or shrimp. The uses are endless. Store it in the fridge or the freezer.

red potato salad

serves 6

Most potato salads are dressed with mayonnaise and tend to be a pretty heavy side dish. These potatoes dress up with a vinaigrette instead. Potato salads are a favorite of church suppers and luncheons. Since the dressing is oil and vinegar, this one is safe to leave at room temperature on those long buffet tables.

1½ pounds small red potatoes, cut in half
2 tablespoons red wine vinegar
½ teaspoon Dijon mustard
1 clove garlic, minced
Juice of 1 lemon

1 tablespoon chopped fresh thyme
¾ teaspoon salt
¼ teaspoon freshly ground black pepper
¼ cup olive oil
Lemon slices, for garnish

In a stockpot, cover the potatoes with cold water and bring to a boil. Boil them for 10 minutes, or until they are tender when tested with a fork.

Meanwhile, whisk together the vinegar, mustard, garlic, lemon juice, thyme, salt, and pepper. While whisking, slowly pour the olive oil into the vinegar mixture.

Drain the potatoes and place in a large serving bowl. Add the dressing and toss lightly, being careful not to break up the potatoes. Garnish the salad with the lemon slices.

baby spinach salad with blueberry and lime vinaigrette

serves 6

The combination of sweet strawberries, salty feta cheese, and the tart dressing makes an incredible salad. I like to serve salads on platters to show off the beautiful colors. Blueberries naturally contain pectin, so the dressing will become thick if it sits for a while. If you need to, whisk in a little more olive oil to thin it out.

1 (6-ounce) package baby spinach
1 cup sliced strawberries
1 cup crumbled feta cheese
1 cup fresh blueberries
¼ cup white balsamic vinegar

Zest of 1 lime
1 tablespoon freshly squeezed lime juice
1 tablespoon honey
⅔ cup olive oil

Arrange the spinach on a serving platter. Top with the strawberries and feta cheese.

For the dressing, place the blueberries, vinegar, lime zest and juice, and honey in the bowl of a food processor fitted with a metal blade. Process until the blueberries are pureed, about 1 minute. With the food processor running, slowly add the olive oil in a steady stream.

Drizzle the dressing over the salad and serve.

dilled cucumber soup

makes 7½ cups

chilling time: 1 hour

With summer days in the South often reaching above 90°F, chilled soups are a blessing. This soup is creamy and satisfying while still refreshing. Add a piece of crusty bread for an unforgettable lunch.

4 cups chopped, seeded, and peeled
  cucumbers
1 small Vidalia onion, chopped
2 avocados, chopped
2 tablespoons freshly squeezed lemon juice

3 cups chicken broth
1 (8-ounce) container sour cream
¼ teaspoon freshly ground black pepper
1 tablespoon white wine vinegar
1 tablespoon chopped fresh dill

Place the cucumbers, onion, avocados, and lemon juice in the bowl of a food processor fitted with the metal blade. Process until the cucumbers are pureed, about 1 minute.

Transfer the mixture to a large mixing bowl. Add the chicken broth, sour cream, pepper, vinegar, and dill and whisk to combine.

Chill the soup for at least 1 hour before serving.

real tomato soup

makes 4½ cups

Tomato soup is not tomato soup when it's made with canned tomatoes. Using fresh, ripe tomatoes doesn't have to mean a long time at the stove. Skipping the peeling and seeding is one way to save a large amount of prep time. The soup is pureed before serving, so all the nutrition of the peel is blended right in.

2 tablespoons olive oil
1 medium Vidalia onion, finely chopped
2 cloves garlic, minced
1 cup chicken broth
2¼ pounds tomatoes, chopped

1 teaspoon salt
½ teaspoon freshly ground black pepper
½ cup heavy whipping cream
1 tablespoon chopped fresh oregano
1 tablespoon chopped fresh basil

Heat the olive oil in a stockpot over medium heat. Add the onion and cook, stirring, for 5 minutes. Add the garlic and cook for 1 minute.

Add the chicken broth, chopped tomatoes, salt, and pepper. Cover the stockpot and cook for 6 minutes.

Remove from the heat. Use a hand blender to puree the soup right in the stockpot. Or puree in batches with a traditional blender.

Return the stockpot to low heat. Add the cream, oregano, and basil. Cook for 3 more minutes.

cooking school

Keep your kitchen scale clean when weighing ingredients. Lay a piece of plastic wrap over the scale to keep the surface clean.

fast brunswick stew

makes about 17 cups

Ask a Southerner about the origins of Brunswick stew, and you'll start quite the historical debate. Brunswick County in Virginia and Brunswick, Georgia, both lay claim to the first pot of the famous stew. (I, of course, tend to lean toward the Georgia version.) No matter where it came from, family recipes are passed down and sometimes even the pots in which they bubble. I am now the proud keeper of my grandfather's handmade stew pot.

Brunswick stew traditionally takes hours upon hours to make. Sometimes, it even takes days. With so many ingredients usually made from scratch, it can be a true labor of love. With this super-fast version, rotisserie chicken, leftover barbecue, and canned veggies take most of the preparation time out of the stew. The recipe makes a big batch, so portion out some for later and freeze for up to 3 months. Use leftover barbecued pork from page 91 or pick up some at your favorite restaurant.

1 pound lean ground beef
2 (15.25-ounce) cans whole kernel corn or 3 cups frozen kernel corn, thawed
2 (15-ounce) cans sweet peas or 3 cups frozen sweet peas, thawed
2 (14.5-ounce) cans stewed tomatoes with onions and celery
1 (14.75-ounce) can cream-style sweet corn
3 (15-ounce) cans tomato sauce

1 (4.5-ounce) can chopped green chiles
3 cups chopped barbecued pork
2 cups chopped cooked chicken (½ rotisserie chicken)
¼ cup white vinegar
2 tablespoons packed light brown sugar
1 teaspoon hot sauce
Zest and juice of 1 lemon
2 teaspoons salt (see Note)

Brown the ground beef in a large stockpot over medium heat. Use a spatula or a spoon to break up any large clumps as it cooks. Drain the meat and return to the stockpot.

While the beef is browning, drain the cans of whole kernel corn and sweet peas. If canned stewed tomatoes are in large pieces, use a pair of kitchen scissors to chop them slightly, right in the can. Once the beef is browned and drained, add the drained corn, peas, and stewed tomatoes to the ground beef.

Add the cream-style corn, tomato sauce, green chiles, barbecued pork, chicken, vinegar, brown sugar, hot sauce, lemon zest and juice, and salt to the stockpot. Simmer the stew for 15 minutes.

note: The amount of salt is going to depend on the brand of canned items. Some vary more in salt amounts than others. Taste for salt and add as you need it.

chilled strawberry peach soup

makes 4 cups

Serve this soup as a first course for a brunch or lunch. I also like it in shot glasses with a cheese course. Frozen strawberries and peaches also work well when fresh fruit isn't in season. Look for limeade near the fresh orange juice.

1 pound fresh strawberries
1½ pounds fresh peaches
1 cup limeade
2 tablespoons honey, plus more for swirls

Remove the stems from the strawberries. Peel and segment the peaches. Transfer the fruit to the bowl of a food processor fitted with the metal blade. Process for 1 minute, or until completely pureed.

Add the limeade and honey and process until combined.

Transfer the soup to serving bowls. Drizzle each serving with a swirl of honey.

little beet salad

serves 4

If you can't find small beets, cut larger ones into 1-inch pieces. Although harder to find than the typical red, look for beets that are different colors, like white or yellow. Choose the beets with the greens attached.

¾ pound small beets (about the size of a golf ball)
1 cup beet greens
2 tablespoons red wine vinegar
1 teaspoon coarse-grained mustard

⅛ teaspoon ground ginger
1 tablespoon freshly squeezed lemon juice
¼ teaspoon salt
3 tablespoons olive oil
3 cups mixed lettuce leaves

Remove the tops from the beets and peel the beets. Cut each beet into 4 wedges. Steam in a steamer basket for 18 minutes, or until fork-tender.

Meanwhile, choose 1 cup of the smallest of the beet greens, stack the leaves, and slice into ribbons. Set aside.

Whisk together the red wine vinegar, mustard, ginger, lemon juice, and salt. While whisking, slowly pour the olive oil into the vinegar mixture.

Combine the lettuce and sliced beet greens and arrange on a small platter. Toss the warm steamed beets with about half the dressing in a small mixing bowl. Pour the beets over the lettuce. Serve the remaining dressing on the side.

cooking school

Steamer baskets come in just about every color and shape you can imagine. The stainless-steel expandable one that your mom used is still a great choice. I have a silicone steamer basket I like because it has handles for easy lifting out of the pan.

herbed tomato sandwiches

serves 4

I remember sitting at the kitchen table long after lunch with an untouched tomato sandwich on my plate. I must have been about ten years old and was refusing to try the very food that would become the sole reason I now grow tomatoes each summer. Once I appreciated the simple, honest tomato sandwich for the delicacy it is, I was hooked.

Use whatever fresh herbs you have on hand, like basil, oregano, and chives. I still prefer good, old-fashioned white bread for my tomato sandwiches.

1 tablespoon chopped fresh herbs
½ cup mayonnaise
8 slices bread
1 pound tomatoes, cut into ½-inch-thick
   slices

Combine the herbs and the mayonnaise in a small mixing bowl. Spread one side of all the slices of bread with mayonnaise.

Top 4 slices of the bread with tomatoes. Top with the remaining 4 slices.

tarragon chicken tea sandwiches

makes about 50

Tea sandwiches have graced the tables of countless Junior League meetings and garden club get-togethers for generations. Ideal for brunch, lunch, or of course afternoon tea, little sandwiches are perfect for picking up and nibbling while never missing the conversation.

1 rotisserie chicken
1/3 cup mayonnaise
1 tablespoon chopped fresh tarragon
1/4 teaspoon salt

1/8 teaspoon freshly ground black pepper
1/4 teaspoon lemon zest
1 tablespoon finely chopped red onion
35 slices sandwich bread

Remove the skin from the chicken and pull the meat off the bone. Chop the chicken meat into 1/2-inch pieces.

In a large mixing bowl, combine the chicken, mayonnaise, tarragon, salt, pepper, lemon zest, and onion.

Cut the crust off the slices of bread if you prefer. Cut each slice of bread into 3 strips (each about 1 inch wide).

Spread the chicken salad on half of the bread strips. Top with the remaining strips.

egg salad

makes 2 cups

serves 4

The Augusta National is famous for serving two sandwiches while hosting the Masters: egg salad and pimento cheese. Each one is wrapped in green wax paper and is made of white bread so soft it feels good in your hands. I have devoured my fair share while sitting in the grass at the world's most famous golf course. Each time I eat an egg salad sandwich, I think of the tournament.

8 large eggs
½ cup mayonnaise
1 tablespoon Dijon mustard

⅛ teaspoon salt
⅛ teaspoon freshly ground pepper
8 slices sandwich bread

Cover the eggs with about 1 inch of cold water in a large saucepan. Bring the water to a boil over high heat. When the water boils, turn the heat off and let the eggs sit for 10 minutes. Submerge the eggs under cold water. Peel the eggs while holding them in running cold water.

Chop the eggs with an egg slicer or a knife. Combine the chopped eggs, mayonnaise, mustard, salt, and pepper in a medium mixing bowl.

Spread about ½ cup of egg salad on each of 4 slices of bread. Top with the remaining 4 slices.

bltva sandwiches

serves 4

This takes the average BLT to a new level for tomato lovers like me. For a fun addition to lunch, make a "sandwich bar" by arranging all the ingredients buffet style. Then everyone can personalize their own sandwich just the way they like it.

8 slices sandwich bread
¼ cup mayonnaise
1 pound tomatoes, cut into ½-inch-thick
    slices

12 slices cooked bacon
½ large Vidalia onion, sliced into rings
1 avocado, sliced
4 lettuce leaves

Spread one side of each slice of bread with mayonnaise.

Top 4 slices of bread with tomatoes, bacon, onion rings, avocado slices, and lettuce leaves. Top with the remaining 4 slices of bread.

way back when

Many Southerners are very particular about the mayonnaise they use. Duke's Mayonnaise is made in Greenville, South Carolina, and has been a Southern staple for almost 100 years. It's widely available throughout the South. See Resources.

tailgates
and
gatherings

Southerners are known for using any excuse to get together. We'll have a party for just about anything. It may be an intimate dinner party in the dining room or a massive celebration for the Fourth of July, but choosing the right recipes for the occasion is the first step. The guests won't remember the dust on the coffee table, but they will remember what was served and how good it tasted. Make an impression with Brown Butter and Pecan Trout, Dressed-Up Oysters, or Pecan-Crusted Rack of Lamb.

College football is practically a religion in the South. In a college town, tailgates are pretty much the main topic of conversations (other than the game) from September until December. For people like me who have a greater love of food than of the game, tailgating is the most important event occurring on game day. Without a proper tailgate, no fan can be full and happy when the kickoff finally occurs. No tailgate is complete without a batch of Short-Cut Barbecue, Mama's Baked Beans, Grilled Vidalias, or Mustard and Sage Pork Tenderloin.

Truly talented tailgaters are easily spotted with their lavish tables covered in linens and adorned with the family silver. A few tailgates even have bartenders, quality liquors, and beers that don't come in cans. They have enormous tents, grills that arrive hitched to pickup trucks, fresh flowers, and even TVs for watching all the other games. These are the ones you hope to be invited to.

short-cut barbecue

makes 10 cups

serves 10

slow-cooking time: 7 hours

Southern barbecue recipes are endless, with every serious outdoor cook making his or her own version and swearing it's the best. Preparing a smoker (and learning how to work it) can take quite a lot of time. Save some time by plugging in the slow cooker and letting it do the work. Use the shredded meat to make barbecue sandwiches or combine it with a slice of white bread and slaw for a barbecue plate. If a 6-pound roast is hard to find, use two smaller ones instead.

¼ cup packed light brown sugar
1 tablespoon salt
1 teaspoon celery seed
1 tablespoon chili powder
½ teaspoon cayenne pepper
1 tablespoon paprika

½ teaspoon garlic powder
½ teaspoon freshly ground black pepper
1 (6-pound) bone-in Boston butt roast
1 (12-ounce) pale ale beer
Tangy Barbecue Sauce (page 9)

Lightly spray a 6-quart slow cooker with nonstick cooking spray.

To make the dry rub, combine the sugar, salt, celery seed, chili powder, cayenne, paprika, garlic powder, and pepper in a small bowl. Generously massage the dry rub into all sides of the roast. Place the roast, fat side up, in the prepared slow cooker. Pour the beer around, not over, the roast and place the cover on the slow cooker. Cook on high for 7 hours, or until the meat falls off the bone.

Transfer the roast to a large mixing bowl, discarding the cooking liquid left in the slow cooker. Discard the bones. Use two forks to shred the meat. Stir in 1 cup of Tangy Barbecue Sauce. Serve the remaining sauce on the side.

ribeyes with bourbon pecan butter

serves 4

chilling time: 1 hour

There's no other cut of steak I'd rather eat than a ribeye. The steak is a slice off the rib section and has the perfect marriage of tenderness and flavor. Make sure the butcher leaves the lip (sometimes called the cap) on the steak. It's my favorite part because it's more fatty than the rest of the steak and incredibly tender.

Pecan Bourbon Butter
½ cup unsalted butter
2 tablespoons finely chopped toasted
    pecans (page 8)
½ teaspoon bourbon
⅛ teaspoon salt
⅛ teaspoon freshly ground black pepper
1 teaspoon chopped fresh flat-leaf parsley

4 ribeye steaks, 1 inch thick, about
    ¾-pound each
2 tablespoons olive oil
Salt
Freshly ground black pepper

To make the Pecan Bourbon Butter, combine the butter, pecans, bourbon, salt, pepper, and parsley in a small mixing bowl. Transfer to a sheet of plastic wrap and shape into a 3½-inch log. Chill for 1 hour.

Rub both sides of the steaks with olive oil. Season with salt and pepper.

Heat a cast-iron skillet over medium heat. Cook the steaks for about 4 minutes on the first side and 3 minutes on the second side for medium-rare.

Transfer the steaks to a plate. Top each steak with a ¼-inch-thick slice of Pecan Bourbon Butter. Allow the steaks to rest for at least 5 minutes before serving.

cooking school

Always take meat off the heat when it's about 10 degrees lower than the desired serving temperature. The temperature will rise as the meat rests.

serving temperatures for beef:
130°F Rare
140°F Medium-rare
150°F Medium
160°F Well-done

dressed-up oysters

makes 18 oysters

Oysters beds dot the coast of much of the South. Oysters are a big business and an even greater delicacy. Some people slurp them down raw, others cook them to perfection. You'll need an oyster knife and an old kitchen towel or glove ready for prying open the shells.

6 ounces bacon, chopped
1 shallot, finely chopped
2 tablespoons white wine vinegar

1½ dozen oysters on the halfshell
1 tablespoon chopped fresh flat-leaf parsley
Ice-cream salt, for garnish

Move the oven rack to a position about 5 inches from the broiler. Preheat the broiler.

In a small skillet, cook the bacon over medium heat until browned and crispy. Remove the bacon with a slotted spoon to a paper towel-lined plate, reserving about 1 tablespoon of drippings in the skillet.

Add the shallot to the skillet and cook over medium-low heat for 2 minutes. Add the vinegar and stir to release the browned bits from the skillet. Cook for 30 seconds.

Arrange the oysters on a rimmed baking sheet and broil for 1 to 2 minutes, or until the edges are curled. Spoon the shallot mixture over the oysters and sprinkle with bacon and parsley. Nestle the oyster shells in ice-cream salt to serve.

cooking school

Oysters found in the South are of the Eastern variety. Most of the oysters sold commercially are from the coast along the Gulf of Mexico. They are prized for their sweet and mild flavor.

skirt steak with vidalia onion chimichurri

serves 6

Skirt steaks cook very quickly and are super flavorful. The steaks are long strips about 4 inches wide from the diaphragm muscle. Adding a Southern twist to Argentina's chimichurri sauce dresses the steak up so it's fit for company. The steaks are easily cooked on the grill, too.

½ cup red wine vinegar
½ cup olive oil
4 cloves garlic, smashed
2 pounds skirt steak

½ cup chopped fresh cilantro
¼ cup diced Vidalia onion
2 tablespoons freshly squeezed lemon juice
½ teaspoon kosher salt

Move the oven rack to a position about 5 inches from the broiler. Preheat the broiler.

In a large resealable plastic bag, combine the vinegar, ¼ cup of olive oil, and the garlic cloves. Add the steak to the bag and marinate for 15 minutes.

Meanwhile, to make the chimichurri, combine the cilantro, the remaining ¼ cup of olive oil, onion, lemon juice, and salt in a small bowl. Set aside.

Remove the steaks from the marinade and place them on a rimmed baking sheet. Discard the marinade. Broil for 3 minutes per side. Let the steaks rest for at least 5 minutes before slicing.

Cut each strip of steak in half, to make 2 shorter strips. You can serve the steak this way or in thin strips. For the strips, slice down the long side (across the grain) into ½-inch-thick slices. Serve the chimichurri sauce with the steak.

mustard and sage pork tenderloin

serves 6

marinating time: 4 hours

Serving pork tenderloin to a crowd is a fast and easy way to feed a bunch of friends or fans. This recipe is easily doubled or tripled to satisfy any guest list. Feel free to marinate the pork longer than 4 hours, even as long as a day.

¼ cup olive oil
3 tablespoons apple cider vinegar
1 tablespoon coarse-grained mustard
1 tablespoon finely chopped fresh sage
2 cloves garlic, minced
¼ teaspoon salt
¼ teaspoon freshly ground black pepper
2 (1-pound) pork tenderloins

Creamy Sage Sauce
¼ cup mayonnaise
2 tablespoons milk
2 tablespoons coarse-grained mustard
1 teaspoon finely chopped sage

Combine the olive oil, vinegar, mustard, sage, garlic, salt, and pepper in a small bowl. Trim the silver skin off the pork tenderloins. Place the pork in a large resealable plastic bag and add the marinade. Marinate in the fridge for 4 hours.

To make the Creamy Sage Sauce, whisk together the mayonnaise, milk, mustard, and sage in a small mixing bowl. Chill until serving.

Heat the grill to medium (about 350°F).

Remove the tenderloins from the bag and discard the marinade. Grill the tenderloins, turning to cook all sides, for 20 minutes, or until the meat registers 150°F with a meat thermometer. Let the pork rest for at least 5 minutes before slicing. Serve with Creamy Sage Sauce.

cooking school

The silver skin is a ribbon-like tendon that runs about three quarters of the length of the tenderloin. If cooked, it becomes very tough and rubbery. Slip the blade of a very sharp knife underneath the tendon and gently slice it off.

cooking school

Take raw meat out to the grill on a pan or platter covered in plastic wrap or foil. After the meat is moved to the grill, uncover the platter and it's clean and ready for when the meat is done.

stuffed and baked chicken

serves 4

baking time: 25 minutes

Removing the bone from a chicken breast allows it to cook faster. Leaving the skin on keeps the meat moist and adds flavor. Ask your butcher to debone your chicken breasts and leave the skin on. This will save you time once you get home. I like to go by the meat department first so I can shop while the butcher is working.

3 ounces country ham
4 ounces goat cheese, softened
1 tablespoon finely chopped fresh sage
1 tablespoon freshly squeezed lemon juice

$\frac{1}{8}$ teaspoon freshly ground black pepper
4 boneless chicken breasts, skin on
1 tablespoon olive oil

Preheat the oven to 425°F.

Finely dice the ham. Heat a small frying pan over medium heat. Add the ham and cook for 4 to 5 minutes, or until slightly browned.

Meanwhile, combine the goat cheese and sage in a small mixing bowl.

Remove the skillet from the heat and add the lemon juice to the pan. Scrape up any browned bits from the bottom of the pan with a silicone spatula or wooden spoon. Add the ham and pan drippings to the goat cheese. Stir in the pepper.

Place the chicken breasts on a rimmed baking sheet. Stuff an even amount of goat cheese mixture under the skin of each chicken breast. Rub the olive oil on top of the skin.

Bake at 425°F for 25 minutes, or until the skin is browned.

blackened catfish

serves 4

I like blackened fish when the spice isn't so dominant that it overpowers the taste of the fish. Opt for the larger amounts of cayenne pepper and chili powder if you have tougher taste buds than I do.

½ teaspoon ground cumin
½ teaspoon salt
½ teaspoon ground dried thyme
1 teaspoon dried oregano
½ to ¾ teaspoon cayenne pepper

1 teaspoon dry mustard
1 teaspoon paprika
½ to ¾ teaspoon chili powder
3 tablespoons butter
4 fresh catfish fillets (about 1¼ pounds)

Combine the cumin, salt, thyme, oregano, cayenne pepper, dry mustard, paprika, and chili powder in a small bowl.

Melt 2 tablespoons of the butter in the microwave. Brush both sides of the catfish fillets with the melted butter. Generously sprinkle the catfish fillets with the spice mixture. Rub in gently to coat the fillets.

Heat a large cast-iron skillet over medium heat. Add the remaining 1 tablespoon of butter to the hot skillet. Gently place 2 fillets in the skillet. Cook for 3 to 4 minutes per side, or until the catfish flakes with a fork. Repeat with the remaining 2 fillets.

cooking school

Almost all American farm-raised catfish are raised in the South. This sustainable Southern swimmer is available at most seafood counters.

pecan-crusted racks of lamb

serves 6

roasting time: 25 minutes

If the lamb racks don't already have the ribs cleaned of meat and fat, ask your butcher to french the bones for you. I like to use sage, oregano, and thyme for the chopped herbs. Feel free to use whatever herbs you have on hand.

2 (1½-pound) racks of lamb, frenched
½ cup pecan halves
2 cups loosely packed fresh mint leaves
¼ cup loosely packed fresh herbs
2 cloves garlic, minced

½ teaspoon salt
½ teaspoon freshly ground black pepper
1 teaspoon lemon zest
⅓ cup olive oil

Preheat the oven to 450°F. Line a rimmed baking sheet with aluminum foil.

Place the racks of lamb on the prepared baking sheet. The racks should be lying down with the bones curving toward the bottom of the pan.

Finely chop the pecans, mint leaves, and herbs. Place the pecans and minced herbs in a medium mixing bowl. Add the garlic, salt, pepper, and lemon zest. Stir in the olive oil.

Using half of the herb mixture for each rack, spread the mixture on top of the racks. Pat the herb mixture gently so as to coat the entire top side.

Bake at 450°F for 25 minutes, or until a meat thermometer registers 130°F for medium-rare. Let the lamb rest at least 5 minutes before carving. To carve, slice between each bone.

cooking school

If you haven't tasted lamb in years, you should try it again. Thanks to new farming practices, lamb tastes a lot less gamey than it did a few decades ago.

brown butter and pecan trout

serves 4

Being married to an avid fisherman comes with some delightful perks. Spending cool autumn afternoons in the North Georgia mountains is one of them. I've relaxed on the banks of a stream so filled with trout that it was hard to tell if I was seeing spotted rocks jiggling with the current or plump tasty fish just beneath the surface. Needless to say, we eat very well on those nights. Don't worry about the scales. They are so tiny on a trout, they don't need to be removed.

2 cups pecans
Dash of cayenne pepper
4 rainbow trout fillets
¼ teaspoon salt

⅛ teaspoon freshly ground black pepper
3 tablespoons unsalted butter
1 tablespoon freshly squeezed lemon juice

Place the pecans and cayenne pepper in a food processor fitted with a metal blade. Pulse 10 times. Transfer the pecans to a large plate.

Sprinkle the trout fillets with the salt and pepper. Coat both sides of the fillets with the pecans.

Heat 2 tablespoons of the butter in a large nonstick skillet over medium-low heat. Add 2 trout fillets, skin side up, to the hot skillet.

Cook for about 4 minutes, or until browned. Carefully flip and cook for about 2 more minutes. Remove from the skillet and place on a serving platter.

Add the remaining 1 tablespoon of butter to the skillet. Cook the remaining 2 fillets. Transfer the fillets to the serving platter.

Remove the skillet from the heat and add the lemon juice. Using a wooden or silicone spatula, scrape up any browned bits from the bottom of the pan. Pour over the fillets and serve immediately.

cooking school

Stacking nonstick skillets can scratch the inside of the pans. To prevent scratches, place paper plates inside each skillet before they are stacked.

oyster dressing

serves 6

Oyster Dressing, also called creamed oysters, is a very traditional side dish for holidays and dinner parties in the South. Over the generations, many chafing dishes have been filled with this sinful, briny goodness. Draining the oysters well is key to the creamiest outcome. Once the dish is under the broiler, do not walk away or it will burn before you know it.

Some cooks top the dish with bread crumbs and some opt for saltines. Another option is to leave off the topping and serve a scoop of the dressing over toasted bread for a knife-and-fork appetizer.

3½ ounces shiitake mushrooms
2 green onions
6 tablespoons butter
1 pint oysters, well drained
3 tablespoons all-purpose flour

1½ cups milk
½ cup grated Parmesan cheese
¼ teaspoon cayenne pepper
½ teaspoon salt
4 ounces (1 sleeve) saltine crackers

Move the oven rack to a position about 5 inches from the broiler. Preheat the broiler.

Remove the mushroom stems and coarsely chop the mushroom caps. Slice the green onions. Melt 1 tablespoon of the butter in a large skillet over medium heat. Add the mushrooms and cook for 2 minutes. Add the onions and cook until soft, about 4 minutes. Add the oysters. Cook for 5 minutes, stirring occasionally.

Melt 3 tablespoons of the butter in a large stockpot over medium heat. Add the flour and cook for 1 minute, stirring constantly. Slowly stir in the milk. Cook until thickened, about 3 to 4 minutes. Add the cheese, cayenne pepper, and salt.

Using a slotted spoon, transfer the oyster mixture to the cheese sauce. Transfer to a 2-quart broiler-safe baking dish.

Crush the crackers and arrange over the top of the oyster mixture. Melt the remaining 2 tablespoons of butter and drizzle over the crackers.

Broil for about 2 minutes, or until browned.

mama's baked beans

serves 4 to 6

baking time: 40 minutes

Baked beans have never tasted so good. With the bacon on top and beans bubbling in brown sugar, most tailgaters can't deny a second helping. If you think you don't like baked beans, you haven't had these. I grew up with these beans at each and every summer family holiday. If the grill was fired up, these beans were in the oven. They are still Mama's signature dish.

1 (28-ounce) can bacon and brown sugar
   baked beans, drained
½ cup ketchup
½ cup packed light brown sugar

2 tablespoons Worcestershire sauce
½ cup finely diced white onion
4 to 5 slices bacon (about 5 ounces)

Preheat the oven to 375°F.

Combine the beans, ketchup, brown sugar, Worcestershire sauce, and onion in a medium mixing bowl. Pour the beans into a lightly greased 9 by 9-inch baking dish. Top the beans with the bacon slices.

Bake at 375°F for 40 minutes, or until the bacon is done.

grilled vidalias

serves 4

This unbelievably easy side dish is ideal for tossing on the grill beside a juice steak or barbecued chicken. Thanks to marinating in a reseable plastic bag, there's almost no cleanup. Using white balsamic vinegar keeps the onions at their natural color.

3 medium Vidalia onions (about 1½ pounds)
⅓ cup white balsamic vinegar
⅓ cup olive oil

1½ teaspoons salt
¾ teaspoon freshly ground black pepper

Heat a grill to medium-high (about 400°F).

Cut the stem ends off and peel the onions. Cut the onions into 6 wedges, leaving the roots intact. Transfer the wedges to a resealable plastic bag. Add the vinegar, olive oil, salt, and pepper to the bag. Marinate the onions for 10 minutes.

Grill the onions for 12 minutes, turning once.

cooking school

Leaving the onion roots intact will keep the layers from separating.

chapter 8

busy weeknight suppers

I am the mother of two young children, a wife, a working woman, a daughter, a friend, a sister, a volunteer, and it seems any other role that needs filling. Needless to say, I know the necessity of a busy weeknight supper. Between bath times, deadlines, homework, sports, and supper, putting a meal on the table you can be proud of is an art all in itself.

Recipes like Oats and Bacon Meat Loaf, Southern Pesto with Pasta, and Spicy Mustard Greens will make your weekdays go more smoothly. If dinner can be done or in the oven with no supervision needed, you can be free to attend to all the other 8,000 things you need to do.

With Soft Catfish Tacos and Divine Chicken and Dumplings, the kids will be happy and delightfully full too. Cooking after work or playdates is easier with a little help from everyone in the house. Have the little ones set the table, clean as you go in the kitchen, and most important, use those moments together to have a bit of quality time on a busy weeknight.

soft catfish tacos

makes 6 tacos

Supper doesn't get much fresher and more flavorful than these tacos. Loaded with fresh veggies and tangy lime juice, the salsa is extraordinary on its own too. If you cannot find catfish, try tilapia or another firm, white fish.

6 (6-inch) flour tortillas
1 cup chopped tomato
1 Hass avocado, chopped
1 teaspoon lime zest
1 tablespoon freshly squeezed lime juice
2 tablespoons finely chopped red onion
2 cloves garlic, minced
3 tablespoons chopped fresh cilantro

¼ cup pickled jalapeños, drained and chopped
½ teaspoon salt
1 pound catfish fillets
2 cups shredded lettuce, for serving
Shredded Cheddar cheese, for serving
Sour cream, for serving

Peheat the oven to 350°F.

Wrap the tortillas in foil and warm in the oven for 10 to 15 minutes, or until heated.

Meanwhile, make the salsa. Mix the tomato, avocado, lime zest and juice, onion, garlic, cilantro, jalapeños, and salt in a medium mixing bowl. Set aside.

Place the catfish fillets in single layer on a rimmed baking sheet.

Move the oven rack to a position about 5 inches from the broiler. Preheat the broiler. You can move the tortillas to the bottom rack of the oven to keep them warm.

Broil the catfish for 6 to 8 minutes, or until it flakes easily when tested with a fork. The pan will have some liquid that was released from the fish. Cut the catfish into strips.

Top each tortilla with ⅓ cup of lettuce and then the fish strips. Top the tacos with the salsa and shredded cheese. Serve with sour cream.

cooking school

Finding a perfectly ripe avocado in the grocery store is sometimes hard. Try to shop for the creamy green fruit a couple of days before you need it. That way, you'll have time for it to ripen. They ripen faster in a paper bag. Look for ones that are slightly soft to the touch. If the stem pops off easily and reveals a green spot, it's probably ripe.

green beans and red potatoes

serves 8 to 10

Stringing and snapping beans and shelling peas used to be a family affair. The beans were easier, so I always tried to call dibs on those first. Three generations of the women in our family (my sister and I being the youngest) would sit on the back porch and visit while we worked.

It's funny, I now like my beans left whole, without snaps, in more of the French style. I think they're prettier this way (and quicker to prep).

1¼ pounds green beans
1 pound red potatoes
½ medium yellow onion
1 tablespoon olive oil
1 clove garlic, minced

½ cup chicken broth
1 tablespoon coarse-grained mustard
1½ teaspoons white wine vinegar
½ teaspoon salt
¼ teaspoon freshly ground black pepper

Trim the stem ends off the green beans. Cut the potatoes into ½-inch pieces. Slice the onion half into 1-inch pieces.

Heat the olive oil in a stockpot with a lid over medium heat. Add the onion and garlic. Stir constantly and cook for 4 minutes. Add the potato pieces and cook for 1 minute. Add the beans and cook for 1 minute, stirring constantly.

Add the chicken broth to the stockpot and reduce the heat to medium-low. Cover and cook for 10 minutes.

Remove from the heat. Stir in the mustard, vinegar, salt, and pepper.

oats and bacon meat loaf

serves 6

baking time: 60 minutes

I had the unique pleasure of writing a book for Mary Mac's Tea Room in 2005. It was from the cooks at this famous Atlanta restaurant that I learned about adding oats to meat loaf. Many meat loaves have bread crumbs added to help hold the ingredients together. The oats are so much better than bread crumbs and add a richness to the meat that I love.

2 pounds lean ground beef (7% fat)
¾ cup old-fashioned oats
1 cup diced yellow onion
2 cloves garlic, minced
2 eggs

½ cup ketchup
1 tablespoon Worcestershire sauce
½ teaspoon salt
½ teaspoon freshly ground black pepper
2 slices bacon

Preheat the oven to 400°F.

Mix the beef, oats, onion, garlic, eggs, ketchup, Worcestershire sauce, salt, and pepper in a large mixing bowl. Using your hands is the easiest and fastest way to mix.

Pack the beef mixture into a 4½ by 8½-inch loaf pan. Cut the bacon slices into 4-inch pieces so they will fit on top of the meat loaf without hanging over.

Place the loaf pan on a rimmed baking sheet. Bake for 60 minutes or until a meat thermometer registers 160°F.

cooking school

The term *pan* refers to a metal baking pan and the word *baking dish* refers to one made of glass. The two cook very differently and shouldn't be interchanged. Because of the clear sides of the glass dish, food cooks more quickly than if baked in a dark metal pan. If possible, buy both a metal and a glass version of the items you use most.

spicy mustard greens

serves 4

Mustard greens are just about as popular as collards in the South. They have a spicy flavor, reminiscent of mustard. They are often sold at roadside stands and can also be found in grocery stores. If possible, choose the whole bunches instead of the packages of chopped leaves. Cutting the leaves into ribbons drastically shortens the cooking time and keeps the greens from becoming mushy.

3 bunches mustard greens (about 2¼ pounds)
6 ounces andouille sausage

1½ tablespoons butter
2 cloves garlic, minced
¼ teaspoon salt

Remove the mustard leaves from the stems by folding the leaves over lengthwise so the stem can easily be cut off. You should have about 1¼ pounds of leaves. Rinse the leaves by placing them in a large bowl of cold water. Swish the leaves around to remove any dirt.

Lift the leaves from the water and spin them in a salad spinner to dry.

Stack the leaves into piles about 5 inches high. Hold down each stack and slice the leaves into ½-inch strips. Cut the sausage into ½-inch cubes.

Heat the butter over medium-low heat in a large skillet. Add the sausage and cook for 3 minutes, stirring often. Add the garlic and cook for 1 minute.

Add the mustard leaves to the skillet. Using tongs, toss the leaves constantly. Cook for 3 to 4 minutes, or until the leaves are wilted. Add salt and toss. Serve immediately.

cooking school

Andouille sausage is a Cajun specialty that can be found in most large grocery stores. It's smoked and can range from spicy to "set you on fire" heat. If you're new to the sausage, try the least spicy first.

slow cooker pot roast

serves 6

slow-cooking time: 6 hours

Walking in the door after a hectic weekday to the aromas of a fork-tender pot roast that's ready and waiting is amazingly satisfying. Filling a slow cooker with one of my favorite cuts of meat in the morning is the easiest way for me to have a big supper on a busy day. I add the vegetables 2 hours before the meat is done to prevent them from overcooking and becoming mushy.

1 (2½-pound) boneless chuck roast
1 teaspoon salt
½ teaspoon freshly ground black pepper
1½ tablespoons vegetable oil
2 medium white onions

¼ cup red wine
½ pound baby carrots
¾ pound baby new potatoes
2 tablespoons all-purpose flour

Sprinkle the roast on both sides with salt and pepper. Heat the vegetable oil over high heat in a large skillet. Brown the roast on both sides, about 5 minutes per side.

Cut the onions into 8 wedges each. Place the wedges in the bottom of a 6-quart slow cooker. Turn the heat off on the skillet. Remove the roast and place it on top of the onions in the slow cooker. Pour the red wine in the skillet and scrape up the browned bits from the bottom of the pan. Pour the wine over the roast.

Cover the slow cooker and cook on low for 4 hours.

Add the carrots and potatoes to the slow cooker. Cover and cook an additional 2 hours.

Remove the vegetables and meat from the slow cooker, reserving the drippings. Place on a serving platter and cover loosely.

To make the gravy, turn the slow cooker to high. Sift the flour into the drippings. Cook for 5 minutes, stirring constantly. Strain if the gravy looks lumpy.

quail skillet

serves 4

The best way to get your hands on fresh quail is to make friends with a hunter. If that's not going to happen, they are often sold frozen at specialty markets and at some grocery stores. Quail are little birds, so count on two per person. I've made this recipe with dove, too. I just added more birds to the pan.

Vegetable oil
⅔ cup all-purpose flour
½ teaspoon dried oregano
⅛ teaspoon garlic powder
Dash of cayenne pepper

¼ teaspoon salt
⅛ teaspoon freshly ground black pepper
8 (4-ounce) quail
2 cups chicken broth
4 cups cooked rice, for serving

Pour the vegetable oil to a depth of ¼ inch in a 13-inch skillet with a lid. Heat over medium heat until a pinch of flour sizzles when sprinkled in (about 4 minutes).

Meanwhile, combine the flour, oregano, garlic powder, cayenne pepper, salt, and black pepper in a medium mixing bowl. Dredge the quail in the flour, and then reserve the flour.

Add the floured quail to the hot oil and fry for about 5 minutes, turning to brown all sides. Remove the quail to a plate. Turn off the heat and carefully pour off all but about ¼ cup of the hot oil.

Return the skillet to medium-low heat. Add the reserved flour to the remaining ¼ cup oil in the skillet. Stirring constantly to scrape up any browned bits in the pan, cook for 2 minutes. Slowly whisk in the chicken broth. Return the quail to the skillet, reduce the heat to low, and cover and cook for 15 minutes.

Serve with cooked rice.

cooking school

. . . .

Pouring off hot oil is a task to be done with the utmost care. An empty can is the best vessel for capturing the oil. Never pour it down the sink.

southern pesto with pasta

serves 4

In the South we have the ideal ingredients for making our own version of pesto sauce. Pecan trees are abundant in the South. They grow in front yards and embrace tree houses in backyards. I spent hours picking up pecans in our yard for spending money as a girl. I remember filling a thirteen-gallon bucket to the brim with nuts and my dad took them to the local sheller for me. I made what I thought was a fortune—$7.00. To this day, I have an appreciation for those who work to keep us supplied with the trademark nut of the South.

8 ounces dried spaghetti noodles
⅔ cup toasted pecans halves (page 8)
2 ounces Parmigiano-Reggiano cheese
2 cups packed fresh basil leaves
1 cup packed fresh baby spinach leaves

2 tablespoons freshly squeezed lemon juice
¼ teaspoon salt
½ teaspoon freshly ground black pepper
½ cup olive oil

Cook the spaghetti according to the package directions.

Meanwhile, combine the pecan halves and cheese in the bowl of a food processor fitted with a metal blade. Process for about 15 seconds. Add the basil, spinach, lemon juice, salt, and pepper to the food processor. Process until all the ingredients are so finely chopped that the mixture resembles a paste. With the food processor running, slowly add the olive oil in a steady stream.

Drain the spaghetti and transfer it to a serving bowl. Toss the spaghetti with ½ cup of pesto sauce. Reserve the remaining pesto for another use.

cooking school

To store leftover pesto, cover the top of the pesto with a thin layer of olive oil and refrigerate.

divine chicken and dumplings

serves 8

Most recipes for fast chicken and dumplings cut time by using refrigerated dough. I like to take a few minutes to make real dumplings and save the time by using a rotisserie chicken and boxed chicken broth. I only use organic boxed broth. The flavor is much better than the canned broths.

I have made this recipe and fooled my dad, a lifelong fan of chicken and dumplings, into thinking it was completely from scratch. It's so close to the much longer versions, no one will know.

12 cups chicken broth
1 rotisserie chicken
3 cups self-rising flour, plus more for
   countertop
⅛ teaspoon dried sage

⅛ teaspoon dried thyme
¼ teaspoon dried oregano
¼ teaspoon freshly ground black pepper
6 tablespoons Crisco shortening
1 cup milk

Heat the chicken broth over high heat in a large stockpot with a lid. Remove the skin from the chicken and pull the meat off the bone. Shred the chicken meat.

Add the chicken to the broth and bring to a boil.

Meanwhile, combine the flour, sage, thyme, oregano, and pepper to the bowl of a food processor fitted with the metal blade. Pulse 1 time. Add the shortening and pulse 6 times. Add the milk and process until the dough comes together, about 30 seconds.

Remove the dough from the food processor and place on a lightly floured countertop. Use a floured rolling pin to roll the dough to ⅛-inch thickness. Use a pizza cutter to cut into strips about 1 by 3-inches. Drop the strips into the boiling broth a few at a time. The dumplings will look waterlogged and gooey. Stir very gently just once. Reduce the heat to medium.

Cover and simmer for 25 minutes.

roasted acorn squash

serves 4

Winter squash is so easy for busy nights because you can keep it around for when you need a fill-in side dish. It can be kept at room temperature for several weeks. Add a rotisserie chicken and a salad for dinner in minutes.

2 (1½-pound) acorn squashes
1½ tablespoons olive oil
¼ teaspoon salt

¼ teaspoon freshly ground black pepper
⅛ teaspoon cayenne pepper

Preheat the oven to 450°F.

Cut the squashes in half. Use a spoon to scoop out the seeds and discard. Cut the squashes into 1-inch-thick slices.

Cut each slice into fourths (to create 4 semicircles).

Arrange the squash slices on a rimmed baking sheet and toss with the olive oil.

Combine the salt, black pepper, and cayenne pepper in a small bowl. Sprinkle the spices over the squash. Bake for 15 minutes. Turn the slices over and bake for 10 more minutes.

sausage, vidalias, and tomatoes

serves 6

The South is known for its sausage. Different areas of the South are home to an array of sausages almost as distinct as Southerners themselves. I've often made this recipe with venison sausage. It's a great way to use what you have in the freezer. I go a little overboard, but I like to keep a shelf stocked with our favorite sausages. I especially like to make this recipe on cold winter nights. During the summer months, use fresh tomatoes instead.

2 tablespoons olive oil
1½ pounds Italian-style sausage
1 medium Vidalia onion, sliced into half-moons
1 clove garlic, minced

1 (28-ounce) can chopped tomatoes
2 tablespoons chopped fresh basil
½ teaspoon salt
¼ teaspoon freshly ground black pepper
6 cups cooked rice, for serving

Heat the olive oil in a large stockpot over medium heat. Add the sausage and cook for 5 minutes. Turn the sausage and cook for an additional 5 minutes.

Using tongs, remove the sausage to a cutting board and slice into 1-inch pieces. Return the sausage to the hot pan. Add the onion and garlic to the pan. Cook for 4 minutes. Add the tomatoes, basil, salt, and pepper. Simmer for 5 minutes.

Serve over cooked rice.

cooking school

Before storing leftovers, lightly spray plastic storage containers with nonstick cooking spray. This prevents tomato sauces from staining them pink.

fresh corn and tomatoes

serves 6

When fresh corn is in season, buy it! The sweet kernels right off the cob are so much better than canned corn, it's hard to ever go back. The next best option is frozen corn. Silver Queen is my favorite variety and is sometimes also available in the freezer case. I like to use basil and oregano, but any fresh herbs will work.

5 ears fresh corn
2 tablespoons unsalted butter
1 clove garlic, diced
1 large Vidalia onion, diced
2 tablespoons heavy cream

1 large tomato, chopped
¼ teaspoon salt
⅛ teaspoon freshly ground black pepper
1 tablespoon chopped fresh herbs

Using a paring knife, cut the kernels away from the ears of corn. Run the back of the knife down the cob to extract as much liquid (called "milk") as possible. Set the corn kernels aside.

In a large skillet, melt the butter and add the garlic and onion. Cook for about 3 minutes. Add the reserved corn kernels and cook for 8 minutes. Stir in the cream. Add the tomato and cook for 5 minutes. Stir in the salt, pepper, and herbs.

cooking school

Pull back the top of the husk to check for plump, tightly packed kernels. The lighter in color the silk, the fresher the corn. A clean, dry toothbrush is the easiest way to remove the silk.

comforting
casseroles

It would be hard to find a kitchen below the Mason-Dixon line without a 9 by 13-inch baking dish. It's as standard down here as a fork and spoon. Things move a little slower in the South and casseroles are no exception. They are the epitome of slow food. But I've made them quicker and simpler with a few easy shortcuts for time-tested classics.

Dive into the baked and bubbly side of Southern cooking with recipes like Shrimp and Grits Bake and Chicken Boudine. The tradition of making casseroles in the South is kept alive with Mozzarella Corn Spoon Bread, Warm Curried Fruit, and Country Ham and Swiss Casserole.

Casseroles are sacred in the South. A properly raised Southerner never consoles a friend in grief without a warm dish filled with creamy comfort. Whether for a sickness, a death, or just a hardship, casseroles deliver tasteful aid, one spoonful at a time.

For many cooks, their casserole recipes have been in their families for generations and are kept under lock and key as part of the family jewels. Especially in small towns, the best casseroles are talked about with the love of an old friend. If a favorite recipe dies with a cook, both are often mourned for years to come.

Shared with a neighbor or served at home, casseroles give Southerners everywhere what we love most—a good excuse to gather at the table.

petite chicken and wild rice casseroles

serves 8

baking time: 30 minutes

This old, traditional Southern casserole has been on dining room tables for generations. I've made it much faster with rotisserie chicken and rice that's already cooked. Use leftover cooked rice when you have it. If you don't, the ready-to-serve packets take just a few minutes to prepare. Don't worry if you don't have enough ramekins. Make it as one big casserole in a 7 by 11-inch baking dish and bake it for 30 minutes. Some cooks like to top it with grated cheese.

1 rotisserie chicken
3 cups cooked long-grain and wild rice or
  2 (8.8-ounce) packs ready-to-serve long-
  grain and wild rice, cooked according to
  package directions
1 tablespoon unsalted butter
¾ cup diced red onion
¼ cup diced celery

1 (8.5-ounce) can quartered artichoke
  hearts, drained
1 cup sour cream
½ cup chicken broth
¾ teaspoon salt
¼ teaspoon freshly ground black pepper
1½ teaspoons curry powder

Preheat the oven to 350°F. Lightly spray 8 (8-ounce) ramekins with nonstick cooking spray.

Remove the skin from the chicken and pull the meat off the bone. Use your fingers to shred the meat by pulling it apart in strips. Place the meat in a large mixing bowl.

Add the rice.

Heat the butter over medium heat in a small frying pan. Add the red onion and celery and cook for 5 minutes, stirring often.

Stir the onion and celery, artichoke hearts, sour cream, chicken broth, salt, pepper, and curry powder into the chicken. Spoon into the prepared ramekins. Place all of the ramekins on a rimmed baking sheet.

Bake for 30 minutes.

double cheese macaroni and cheese

serves 6

baking time: 25 minutes

Drop in any "meat and three" restaurant for some good Southern country cooking and you are guaranteed to find macaroni and cheese. You may find it with bread crumbs on top, custard inside, cheese baked in or cheese on top, or more fancy versions with red peppers and onions. There's only one true requirement: It has to be homemade.

2 cups uncooked macaroni noodles (about ½ pound)
4 ounces white Cheddar cheese
4 ounces sharp Cheddar cheese
¼ cup unsalted butter

¼ cup all-purpose flour
1½ cups milk
½ cup heavy cream
½ teaspoon salt

Preheat the oven to 350°F.

Cook the macaroni according to the package directions.

As the macaroni cooks, grate the cheeses.

Melt the butter in a stockpot over medium-low heat. Add the flour and cook for 1 minute, stirring constantly. Add the milk and cream and cook for 4 minutes, stirring constantly. Remove the pot from the heat and stir in the cheeses and salt.

Drain the macaroni and stir into the cheese sauce. Pour into an 8 by 8-inch baking dish.

Bake for 25 minutes.

chicken spinach burritos

serves 16 (makes 2 casseroles)

baking time: 20 minutes

Mexican food has had some influence on new Southern food. Thanks to our neighbors to the south, we've learned to spice up our cooking with flavors and ingredients that our grandparents didn't know. This recipe makes two casseroles, so it's perfect for saving one and taking one. Or pop one in the freezer for later. Thaw it overnight and bake it for 40 minutes. If you only need one, heat the extra filling and serve as a warm dip with tortilla chips.

1 rotisserie chicken
1 (10-ounce) package frozen chopped
    spinach, thawed and drained well
1 (10-ounce) can tomatoes and green chiles,
    drained
1 cup small curd cottage cheese

1½ cups sour cream
½ teaspoon salt
¼ cup pickled jalapeño slices, diced
4 cups preshredded Mexican cheese blend
18 (6-inch) flour tortillas

Preheat the oven to 350°F. Lightly spray 2 (9 by 13-inch) baking dishes with nonstick cooking spray.

Remove the skin from the chicken and pull the meat off the bone. Use your fingers to shred the meat by pulling it apart in strips.

Stir together the chicken, spinach, tomatoes and green chiles, cottage cheese, sour cream, salt, jalapeños, and 1½ cups of cheese in a large mixing bowl.

Spoon about ¼ cup of the mixture down the center of each flour tortilla. Roll up and place, seam side down, in the prepared baking dishes. Sprinkle half of the remaining cheese (1¼ cups per casserole) on top of each dish.

Bake for 20 minutes, or until lightly browned.

cooking school

Thoroughly drain thawed frozen spinach by squeezing between several layers of paper towels. Squeeze until no liquid remains.

herbed squash casserole

serves 6 to 8

baking time: 30 minutes

2 pounds yellow squash
1 large egg
½ cup mayonnaise
1 tablespoon finely chopped fresh chives
1 tablespoon chopped fresh basil

½ teaspoon chopped fresh thyme
½ teaspoon salt
¼ teaspoon freshly ground black pepper
1¼ cups preshredded sharp
 Cheddar cheese

Preheat the oven to 350°F.

Slice the squash into ½-inch-thick slices. Steam the squash for 12 minutes, or until tender when pierced with a fork.

While the squash is steaming, mix the egg, mayonnaise, chives, basil, thyme, salt, and pepper in a medium mixing bowl.

Remove the squash from the steamer basket. Add the squash and ¾ cup of cheese to the herbs and stir gently to combine.

Pour into a 7 by 11-inch baking dish and top with the remaining ½ cup of cheese.

Bake for 30 minutes.

cooking school

Store fresh herbs in your fridge just like you would flowers in a vase. Place the stems of the herbs in a jar with an inch or two of water. Next, place an open resealable plastic bag over the jar to create the perfect little "greenhouse."

christmas morning soufflé

serves 8

chilling time: overnight

baking time: 1 hour

Mama has served this puffed casserole on every Christmas morning of my life. I can't imagine opening gifts if it wasn't baking away in the oven. She likes to use white sandwich bread, but I've had my say with challah bread instead. It is a traditional Jewish bread made with eggs and has a very airy and light texture.

Because the soufflé is made the night before, breakfast becomes almost effortless. Try it on a weeknight to have breakfast for dinner.

1½ pounds pork sausage
9 eggs
3 cups milk
1½ teaspoons dry mustard
1 teaspoon salt

¼ teaspoon freshly ground black pepper
5 ounces 3-day-old challah bread
1½ cups preshredded sharp
   Cheddar cheese

In a large skillet, cook the sausage over medium heat for about 15 minutes. Stir often to crumble the meat. Remove the sausage and drain on paper towels.

While the sausage is cooking, whisk the eggs in a large mixing bowl. Add the milk, mustard, salt, and pepper.

Cut the bread into 1-inch cubes. You should have 4½ cups of cubes. Stir the bread cubes into the egg mixture. Add the sausage and cheese and stir well.

Lightly spray a 9 by 13-inch baking dish with nonstick cooking spray. Pour the egg mixture into the prepared dish. Cover and chill overnight.

Uncover and bake at 350°F for 1 hour.

chicken boudine

serves 4

baking time: 30 minutes

Chicken Boudine is unique to Athens, Georgia, the town we call home. Mrs. Cobb was a much sought-after caterer who opened her business in 1928. She catered for the best parties in Athens and cooked for seven Georgia governors. Chicken Boudine was one of her signature dishes. Versions of this old recipe vary greatly, but sherry is the signature flavor in every one I've seen. My version is different than the one she served so many years ago, but the sherry is still the star.

2 cups uncooked egg noodles
1 rotisserie chicken
1 tablespoon unsalted butter
1 (8-ounce) package sliced mushrooms
2 green onions, chopped
½ cup diced red bell pepper
⅓ cup dry sherry

1½ cups sour cream
¼ cup chicken broth
¾ teaspoon salt
½ teaspoon freshly ground black pepper
1¾ cups preshredded sharp
   Cheddar cheese

Preheat the oven to 350°F. Lightly spray an 8 by 8-inch baking dish with nonstick cooking spray.

Cook the noodles in boiling water for about 6 minutes and drain.

While the noodles are cooking, remove the skin from the chicken. Pull the meat off the bone. Use your fingers to shred the meat by pulling it apart in strips.

Heat the butter in a large skillet over medium heat. Add the mushrooms and cook, stirring often, for 6 minutes, or until the liquid has evaporated. Add the onions and bell pepper. Cook for 3 minutes. Remove the skillet from the heat and add the sherry. Scrape up any browned bits from the bottom of the pan. Transfer to a large mixing bowl.

Add the noodles, chicken, sour cream, chicken broth, salt, pepper, and 1 cup of cheese to the bowl. Stir well. Pour into the prepared dish. Top with the remaining ¾ cup of cheese.

Bake for 30 minutes.

cooking school
. . . .

Wearing latex gloves while you pull the meat off rotisserie chickens not only keeps your hands clean as you go, but you can simply pull them off for a quick getaway if the phone rings.

mozzarella corn spoon bread

serves 6

baking time: 30 minutes

Spoon bread got its name simply because it was eaten with a spoon. It's a luxurious soufflé-like custard that has the flavor of corn bread with a light and airy texture. Serve it as a side dish or as an entrée for a light lunch. To save the few minutes of cutting kernels off the cob, use 2 cups of thawed frozen corn instead.

Because spoon bread puffs like a soufflé, it falls like a soufflé. Serve it immediately out of the oven to receive the most "oohs and aahs."

4 ears fresh corn (about 2 cups kernels)
2 cups milk
¾ cup yellow cornmeal
2 tablespoons unsalted butter
1 teaspoon salt

½ teaspoon freshly ground black pepper
2 teaspoons chopped fresh thyme leaves
4 large eggs, separated
1 cup preshredded mozzarella cheese

Preheat the oven to 400°F. Lightly spray a 7 by 11-inch baking dish with nonstick cooking spray.

Shuck the corn, remove the silk, and cut the kernels from the cob using a sharp knife. You should have about 2 cups of kernels. In a large saucepan, combine the corn, milk, and cornmeal. Bring to a simmer over medium heat, about 7 minutes, stirring often. The mixture will be very thick. Transfer to a large mixing bowl.

Stir in the butter, salt, pepper, and thyme. Stir in the egg yolks until combined. Stir in the cheese.

Beat the egg whites with a hand mixer for 1 to 2 minutes, or until stiff peaks form. Fold the beaten whites into the cornmeal mixture. Gently pour into the prepared dish.

Bake for 30 minutes, or until puffed and browned. Serve immediately.

spinach and vidalia soufflé

serves 6

baking time: 45 minutes

This impressive casserole is about as versatile as it gets. It works for a meatless main dish, an elegant side, or the star of a luncheon. Using whole milk ricotta cheese really makes the texture creamy and rich. This is not the time to save on calories.

1 medium Vidalia onion
1 tablespoon olive oil
2 (6-ounce) bags baby spinach (about 10 cups)
1 (15-ounce) container whole milk ricotta cheese

4 ounces goat cheese
4 large eggs, beaten
2 tablespoons all-purpose flour
1 teaspoon salt
¼ teaspoon freshly ground black pepper
⅛ teaspoon cayenne pepper

Preheat the oven to 350°F. Lightly spray a 7 by 11-inch baking dish with nonstick cooking spray.

Cut the onion in half and then slice thinly into half-moons. Heat the olive oil in a large skillet over medium heat. Add the onion and cook for 6 minutes, or until soft. Add the spinach and toss with tongs until wilted, about 3 minutes. Transfer to a large mixing bowl. Stir the ricotta, goat cheese, eggs, flour, salt, black pepper, and cayenne pepper into the spinach. Pour into the prepared dish.

Bake for 45 minutes, or until set and puffed.

country ham and swiss casserole

serves 4

baking time: 15 minutes

Many Southern casseroles use macaroni noodles. Orzo, a little rice-shaped pasta, updates this decadent supper option. I think of this casserole as dressed up and have even served it when company's come over. Thanks to the country ham, no salt is needed.

8 cups water
1 bunch thin asparagus (about 10 ounces)
1¼ cups uncooked orzo
½ pound country ham
1½ cups finely chopped sweet onion

1 cup sour cream
1 cup shredded Swiss cheese
1 teaspoon lemon zest
1 tablespoon freshly squeezed lemon juice
¼ teaspoon freshly ground black pepper

Preheat the oven to 350°F. Lightly spray an 8 by 8-inch baking dish with nonstick cooking spray.

Bring 8 cups of water to a boil in a large saucepan. Remove the tough ends of the asparagus and cut the spears into 1-inch pieces. Add to the boiling water and cook for 2 minutes. Remove the asparagus from the water and place in a large mixing bowl, reserving the water in the pan.

Add the orzo to the boiling water and cook for 6 minutes. Drain and add to the asparagus.

Meanwhile, chop the country ham. Cook the ham and onion in a medium skillet over medium-high heat for 8 minutes. Transfer to the mixing bowl with the asparagus and orzo.

Stir in the sour cream, Swiss cheese, lemon zest, lemon juice, and pepper. Pour into the prepared baking dish.

Bake for 15 minutes.

cooking school

Always zest a lemon before squeezing it for juice.

warm curried fruit

serves 6 to 8

baking time: 45 minutes

Sometimes called Hot Curried Fruit, this side dish has been served to generations of Southerners. I like to make it for Thanksgiving. It's wonderful with roasted turkey.

1 (20-ounce) can pineapple chunks in
   100% juice
1 (15-ounce) can pear halves in 100% juice
2 (15-ounce) cans sliced peaches in
   100% juice
¾ cup dried cherries
½ cup dried raspberries
½ cup chopped dried strawberries
⅓ cup chopped pecans

¼ cup unsalted butter
¼ cup packed light brown sugar
1 teaspoon curry powder
1 tablespoon white wine vinegar

Preheat the oven to 375°F. Lightly spray a 7 by 11-inch baking dish with nonstick cooking spray.

Drain the pineapple chunks, pear halves, and sliced peaches and toss the fruit together in a large mixing bowl. Reserve the juice for another use. Add the cherries, raspberries, strawberries, and pecans and stir well.

Pour into the prepared baking dish.

Melt the butter in the microwave. Stir the brown sugar, curry, and vinegar into the hot butter. Pour over the fruit.

Bake for 45 minutes. Serve warm.

cooking school

To clean a can opener, run a damp, folded paper towel through the blades, as you would a can.

shrimp and grits bake

serves 6

baking time: 25 minutes

Shrimp and grits became a favorite of mine while I was living in Charleston, South Carolina, for culinary school. I like to order it when a see it on a menu because every chef makes it differently. Baking it all together in one dish is certainly easier and faster than the traditional recipes.

4 cups chicken broth
1 cup quick grits
4 ounces cream cheese
1 cup preshredded Monterey Jack cheese
1 pound medium shrimp
½ medium red onion
1 tablespoon unsalted butter

1 clove garlic, minced
1 tablespoon chopped fresh parsley
1 tablespoon freshly squeezed lemon juice
½ teaspoon salt
½ teaspoon freshly ground black pepper
½ cup preshredded sharp Cheddar cheese

Preheat the oven to 375°F. Lightly spray a 7 by 11-inch baking dish with nonstick cooking spray.

Combine the broth and grits in a large stockpot. Turn the heat to medium-high and cook for 20 minutes, stirring very often. Remove from the heat and stir in the cream cheese and Monterey Jack.

While the grits are cooking, peel and chop the shrimp. Set aside.

Finely chop the red onion.

Heat the butter in a small skillet. Add the red onion and garlic. Cook for 4 to 5 minutes, or until softened. Stir into the grits.

Add the shrimp, parsley, lemon juice, salt, and pepper to the grits. Stir to combine. Spoon into the prepared dish. Top with the Cheddar cheese.

Bake for 25 minutes.

chapter 10

girls'
night in

The nurturer must be nurtured. Women are insanely busy—working outside the home, raising a family, or both—and we need a night for ourselves as a way to refuel. Women everywhere, not just down South, enjoy spending time with their friends to recharge their batteries for a night that feels like a mini vacation. What better way than to share favorite foods while catching up and empathizing about each other's lives? Visiting over a stack of Fried Green Tomatoes or Mini Buffalo Burgers never tasted so good. Invite the girls over for an evening of laughter, a little gossip, and most important, great food.

This kind of night out makes us think of ourselves as girls, whatever our age, because we feel carefree, relaxed, even a few years younger. Creating the right atmosphere calls for foods that feel special but are quick and easy to prepare, leaving plenty of time for friends and conversation. Make the night easy with foods that are perfectly feminine. Not too much, not too little. Serving Little Crab Cakes, Shrimp and Roasted Red Pepper Quesadillas, or Tomato Biscuit Pie creates a special night for everyone. Great company only makes good food better.

boiled shrimp with old bay sauce

serves 8 to 10

I know—Old Bay hails from, dare I say, Maryland. But boiled shrimp is king in the South and a little spice from the North won't hurt. Watch the shrimp as it boils. Overcooked shrimp is rubbery and tough and no fun for anyone.

1 gallon water
4 dried bay leaves
2 lemons
2 pounds medium shrimp, shells on
1 cup mayonnaise

¼ cup freshly squeezed lemon juice
2 teaspoons Old Bay seasoning
¼ teaspoon hot sauce
2 teaspoons chopped fresh flat-leaf parsley

Bring the water, bay leaves, and slices from 1 lemon to a simmer in a large stockpot. Add the shrimp and cook for 2 to 4 minutes. The cooking time will depend on the size of the shrimp. Remove the shrimp when they are pink and have curled.

Arrange the shrimp on a platter. Cut the remaining lemon into small wedges and serve with the shrimp.

For the sauce, combine the mayonnaise, lemon juice, Old Bay, hot sauce, and parsley in a small mixing bowl. Serve with the shrimp.

cooking school

If at all possible, always purchase wild American shrimp. Wild shrimp are much better for the environment than the imported farmed varieties. Shrimp caught in the South Atlantic have almost a sweet flavor and tend to be very succulent.

roasted tomatoes and parmesan grits

serves 8

I adore roasted tomatoes and I practically live for creamy grits, so one fateful day, I combined my two loves. If I do say so myself, it was a stroke of genius. The two complement each other in total harmonies of texture, flavor, and color.

3 cups chicken broth
2 cups heavy cream
1 cup quick grits
2 cups grape tomatoes
1½ teaspoons olive oil

1 tablespoon balsamic vinegar
¼ cup plus 2 tablespoons shredded
 Parmesan cheese
Freshly ground black pepper

Preheat the oven to 400°F.

Bring the chicken broth and heavy cream to a simmer in a large heavy saucepan over medium-low heat, about 5 minutes. Add the grits. Stirring often, cook for 20 minutes, until the grits are no longer crunchy.

While the grits are cooking, cut the tomatoes in half and place on a rimmed baking sheet. Toss the tomatoes in olive oil and arrange in a single layer. Bake for 15 minutes. Add the balsamic vinegar and toss.

Remove the grits from the heat and stir in the Parmesan cheese. Serve the tomatoes over the grits. Sprinkle with the pepper before serving.

shrimp and roasted red pepper quesadillas

serves 6

Taste the jalapeños before adding. Different brands can pack different levels of heat. Most seafood markets sell shrimp that's already cooked. Some will even cook your shrimp while you shop. It's a big timesaver.

1½ pounds cooked peeled shrimp
1 (12-ounce) jar roasted red peppers, drained
½ cup olive oil
8 (10-inch) flour tortillas

4 cups preshredded Monterey Jack cheese with peppers
1 cup pickled jalapeño peppers, drained
Sour cream

Use a paring knife to cut the shrimp in half. Cut the red peppers into thin strips.

Heat 1 tablespoon of the olive oil in a large nonstick skillet. Place 1 tortilla in the pan. Sprinkle with cheese, shrimp, peppers, and jalapeños. Top with another tortilla.

Once the cheese is melted, carefully turn the quesadilla with a large spatula. Remove it from the pan after it is browned. Repeat with the remaining tortillas.

Slice each quesadilla into 6 wedges and serve with sour cream.

fried green tomatoes

serves 8

If a Southerner says he doesn't like fried green tomatoes, be very wary. One reason we grow so many tomatoes is simply to eat them before they are ready. A green tomato is tart and filling. Serve with a little lettuce and goat cheese for a main course not to be missed.

Vegetable oil
1 cup cornmeal
4 large green tomatoes (about 2 pounds)
1 cup all-purpose flour

1 teaspoon salt
½ teaspoon freshly ground black pepper
2 large eggs
¼ cup buttermilk

In a large skillet, pour the vegetable oil to a depth of ¼ inch. Heat the skillet over medium heat until a pinch of cornmeal sizzles when sprinkled in.

While the oil heats, peel and slice the tomatoes into ½-inch-thick slices.

Combine the cornmeal, flour, salt, and pepper in a large mixing bowl. Combine the eggs and buttermilk in a small mixing bowl.

Coat each tomato slice with the cornmeal mixture; dip thoroughly in the egg mixture, and return to coat a second time in the cornmeal mixture.

Carefully place about half of the coated tomato slices in the hot oil and fry for 3 to 4 minutes per side, or until golden brown. Repeat with the remaining tomato slices.

cooking school

A green tomato is simply a tomato that is unripe. At this stage, they are much more firm and tart than when they ripen, so they hold up well to frying.

mini buffalo burgers

serves 8

Bison, a member of the buffalo family, has been long prized for its earthy flavor and healthy properties. Farms that raise the mighty animal have popped up in many Southern states.

These little burgers are best right off the heat. Because bison is so lean, it's important not to overcook them. Ground bison can be found in most large grocery stores. The label may say *buffalo* or *bison*.

1 pound ground buffalo
½ cup finely diced red onion
¾ cup finely shredded sharp white Cheddar cheese
½ teaspoon salt
¼ teaspoon freshly ground black pepper
4 cups baby arugula
1 teaspoon Dijon mustard
8 small dinner rolls

Move the oven rack to a position about 5 inches from the broiler. Preheat the broiler.

Combine the buffalo, onion, cheese, salt, and pepper. Divide the meat into 8 portions and shape into patties that are about 1 inch thick. Place the patties on a broiler pan and broil for 3½ minutes. Flip the burgers and broil for 1½ minutes more, or until they are browned and sizzling.

Toss the arugula with the Dijon mustard. Top the burgers with the arugula and serve in dinner rolls.

cooking school

Bison is one of the healthiest choices a red meat eater can make. The meat has more iron than beef and less cholesterol and fat than chicken.

butter bean and bacon hummus

makes 5 cups

Everything from boiled peanuts to black-eyed peas is showing up in hummus recipes all over the South. Dried butter beans take hours to soften up, so I like to use the frozen ones instead. Baby lima beans are what Southerners refer to as butter beans. The other limas you'll see in the store are the much larger variety called Fordhooks.

I serve this with just about anything: crackers, sliced tomatoes, celery, and baby carrots.

1 (2-pound) bag frozen baby lima beans
3 slices bacon (about 3 ounces)
3 tablespoons diced Vidalia onion
3 tablespoons olive oil
2 tablespoons freshly squeezed lemon juice

2 tablespoons tahini
¾ teaspoons salt
¼ teaspoon freshly ground black pepper
Chopped fresh chives, for garnish

Cook the beans in boiling water according to the package directions, usually about 25 minutes total. Drain and rinse under cold running water. Drain well again.

While the beans cook, prep all the other ingredients.

Place the bacon slices between layers of paper towels and cook until crisp in the microwave, about 3 minutes. Crumble the slices after they have cooled.

Place the bacon and onion in a food processor fitted with the metal blade. Pulse 3 times. Add the beans, olive oil, lemon juice, tahini, salt, and pepper. Process until smooth, about 1 minute.

Transfer to a serving bowl and garnish with chopped chives.

cooking school

This is the easiest way to get every morsel out of a food processor bowl: First scoop out all you can, then place the bowl and blade back on the machine and pulse 1 to 2 times to get almost all the food off the blade. Remove the blade and use a spatula to remove everything left in the bowl.

tomato panzanella

makes 7 cups

This Southern spin on the traditional bread salad is a great way to use leftover bread. It's best served right away, but all the ingredients can be prepped and combined at the last minute. Be sure to buy kalamata olives that have been pitted. It saves a great deal of time.

2 large tomatoes
½ cup loosely packed fresh basil leaves
6 ounces day-old French bread, torn into
   2-inch pieces
½ cup pitted kalamata olives, cut in half

½ cup toasted pecan halves (page 8)
⅓ cup olive oil
¼ cup balsamic vinegar
½ teaspoon salt
¼ teaspoon freshly ground black pepper

Cut the tomatoes into ½-inch pieces. You should have about 3 cups of tomatoes. Stack up the basil leaves and slice them into very thin ribbons.

In a large serving bowl, combine the tomatoes, basil, bread, olives, pecans, olive oil, balsamic vinegar, salt, and pepper. Stir until the bread is coated with the oil and vinegar.

Serve within 2 hours.

okra fritters

makes 20

Sa made fried okra patties that were to die for. We made the truly regrettable mistake of not writing down the recipe before she passed away. Now, we have the difficult job of cooking and tasting fried okra fairly often, in hopes of getting it just like hers. This version comes very close.

½ pound okra
¾ cup cornmeal
⅓ cup self-rising flour
½ cup plus 2 tablespoons buttermilk

1 large egg
½ teaspoon salt
¼ teaspoon freshly ground black pepper
¼ cup vegetable oil

Cut the okra into ⅛-inch-thick slices. You should have about 2 cups of sliced okra. Combine the cornmeal, flour, buttermilk, egg, salt, and pepper in a large mixing bowl. Whisk until everything is combined. Stir in the okra.

Heat the vegetable oil in a large nonstick skillet over medium-high heat.

Scoop out heaping tablespoons of the okra batter and carefully place in the hot oil. Use the back of a spoon to flatten slightly in the pan. Cook for 2 to 3 minutes per side, or until browned and crispy. Drain on paper towels. Repeat with the remaining batter.

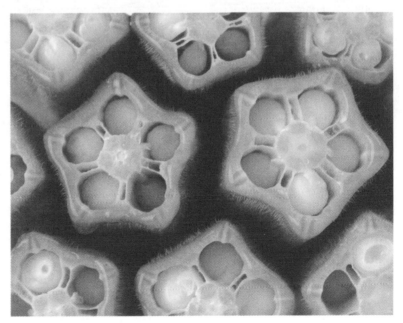

stuffed corn bread

serves 6

If you thought you loved corn bread as much as possible, get ready for a near emotional breakdown. Not only is it beautiful, it tastes amazingly fantastic. Cut it into small wedges for a pickup party food or serve it as a side dish, light entrée, or paired with soup. The possibilities are endless.

Use the extra oil from the tomatoes for making salad dressings or for a dipping sauce for fresh bread.

1 (8.5-ounce) jar sun-dried tomatoes,
    packed in oil
1 cup white cornmeal
¾ cup all-purpose flour
2 teaspoons baking powder
1 teaspoon baking soda
½ teaspoon salt
1 cup milk
1 large egg
1 teaspoon finely chopped fresh rosemary
2 ounces goat cheese, crumbled

Preheat the oven to 425°F.

Drain the sun-dried tomatoes over a small mixing bowl and reserve the oil. Place 2 tablespoons of the reserved oil in a 10-inch cast-iron skillet. Place the skillet in the oven as it preheats. Reserve the remaining oil for another use. Chop the tomatoes.

Combine the cornmeal, flour, baking powder, baking soda, and salt in a medium mixing bowl.

Combine the milk and egg in a small mixing bowl. Stir into the cornmeal mixture. Remove the heated skillet from the oven and pour about half of the hot oil into the batter. It will sizzle and bubble immediately. Stir to incorporate the oil.

Pour about half of the batter into the hot skillet. Sprinkle the tomatoes, rosemary, and goat cheese evenly over the batter. Pour the remaining half of the batter over the stuffing. It will not cover the stuffing completely. Do not spread the batter.

Bake for 18 to 20 minutes, or until golden brown.

cooking school
. . . .

I prefer to use white cornmeal, as do most Southerners, in my cooking. If you can't find white, it's okay to use yellow. Both white and yellow are interchangeable.

little crab cakes

makes 12

On beach trips, we put out our crab traps and like to catch the real thing for supper. It doesn't take long to learn that picking crabmeat from a blue crab is an easy way to build up an appetite.

The crab cakes freeze well before they are cooked. Place them in a single layer on a baking sheet to freeze. Once frozen, store them in a resealable plastic bag. Thaw them in the fridge for several hours and cook as directed.

1 pound fresh claw crabmeat
1 clove garlic, minced
⅓ cup finely diced red bell pepper
2 green onions, thinly sliced
2 tablespoons chopped fresh flat-leaf
   parsley
2 tablespoons mayonnaise

1 tablespoon Dijon mustard
Zest of 1 lemon
½ teaspoon salt
¼ teaspoon freshly ground black pepper
2 eggs, lightly beaten
1 cup bread crumbs
¼ cup unsalted butter

Spread the crabmeat out on a rimmed baking sheet. Run your fingers through the meat to find and remove any shell. Transfer the crab to a medium mixing bowl. Add the garlic, red bell pepper, green onions, parsley, mayonnaise, mustard, lemon zest, salt, pepper, and eggs. Stir in ½ cup of bread crumbs.

Use a ¼-cup dry measuring cup to scoop out the crabmeat mixture. Shape into cakes.

Arrange the remaining ½ cup of bread crumbs on a plate. Dredge the crab cakes in the bread crumbs.

Heat 2 tablespoons of the butter in a large nonstick skillet over medium heat. Add half of the crab cakes and cook for 3 to 4 minutes per side, or until browned. Turn the crab cakes very carefully with a small spatula to avoid breaking them up. Remove from the pan and cook the remaining crab cakes in the remaining 2 tablespoons of butter.

cooking school

Most refrigerated crabmeat in the grocery store is sold pasteurized. It's usually good for about 6 months, so don't be shocked by the sell-by date's being so far in the future. The crabmeat on the canned tuna aisle is not the same quality in flavor or texture. Buy the refrigerated meat instead.

asparagus bundles with bacon

serves 8

Marinating asparagus and wrapping them in bundles with thick, juicy bacon turns the spears into a little entrée or a hefty side dish. Saving the marinade for drizzling over the cooked bundles adds one last punch of flavor. The bundles can also be roasted in the oven.

2 pounds medium asparagus (2 bunches)
⅓ cup balsamic vinegar
1 clove garlic, minced

½ teaspoon dried thyme leaves
⅛ teaspoon freshly ground black pepper
8 slices thick-cut bacon

Preheat the grill to medium heat (about 350°F).

Remove the tough ends of the asparagus.

Combine the balsamic vinegar, garlic, thyme, and pepper in a large shallow dish. Add the asparagus and toss to coat. Marinate at room temperature for 15 minutes. Reserve the marinade.

Bundle about 8 or 9 spears together and wrap in bacon. The bacon will hold the spears together without any toothpicks or skewers. Continue with the remaining asparagus and bacon. You should have 8 bundles.

Grill the bundles for 8 minutes, turning 3 times, or until the bacon is done and the asparagus is tender. Transfer the bundles to a serving platter and drizzle with the reserved marinade.

tomato biscuit pie

serves 6 to 8

baking time: 20 minutes

cooling time: 5 minutes

This extremely rich combination of two Southern icons is unforgettable. With the crust made from a quick biscuit dough and topped with ripe tomatoes, it's quite the crowd pleaser. Serve it as a light entrée or side dish. The crust cooks much better in a metal pan than the same-size glass baking dish.

1 cup butter
2 cups Southern Self-Rising Flour (page 7)
1 (8-ounce) container sour cream
2¼ pounds tomatoes
½ teaspoon salt

½ teaspoon freshly ground black pepper
¼ cup chopped fresh basil
2 tablespoons chopped fresh chives
1½ cups preshredded sharp Cheddar cheese

Preheat the oven to 425°F. Line a 9 x 9-inch pan with aluminum foil. Allow a few inches of foil to overlap on the sides of the pan. Lightly spray the foil with nonstick cooking spray.

Melt the butter in the microwave. Combine the butter, flour, and sour cream in a medium mixing bowl. Spread the dough evenly in the bottom of the prepared pan.

Bake for 20 minutes.

While the crust is baking, peel the tomatoes and slice into ¼-inch-thick slices.

Remove the crust from the oven. It will not be brown, but it will be set. Being careful of the hot pan, arrange half of the tomato slices over the crust. Sprinkle with half of the salt and pepper, half of the basil, half of the chives, and half of the cheese. Repeat the layers.

Bake for 20 more minutes. Let the pie sit for 5 minutes before cutting. For easy cutting and serving, use the foil to lift the pie out of the pan.

cooking school

Turn a baking pan upside down and lay a piece of foil over the pan. Mold the foil over the bottom of the pan. Turn the pan right side up—the foil should slip right in the pan.

southern
sweets

Come dessert time, it's great to sit back, get comfortable, open the windows, and listen to the crickets and cicadas outside. With fork or spoon in hand and something sweetly Southern on the plate, just about any table can be transported to the land of peach trees and sugar cane. Classic tempting recipes like Lazy Girl Berry Cobbler, Real Fast Pralines, and Upside-Down Chess Pies are impossible to resist.

Indulging in desserts is a favorite pastime in the South. Making ice cream on the back porch was always a treat for my sister and me when we were little. On days it was so hot that all we could do was dance in the water hose, we could always hear the whine and grind of the ice-cream machine running in the background. The minute it was frozen enough to stand up on a spoon, we maneuvered our tiny hands to get to the peaches and frozen cream. Mm . . . it was so, so good.

Be proud of your newfound Southern heritage by serving sweets that take minutes to prepare but taste like you cooked for hours. Get your chocolate fix with Double Chocolate Scoop Pie or pucker up for Mini Key Lime Tarts. There's nothing quite like a sweet ending.

benne seed sugar cookies

makes 20 cookies

Sesame seeds are known as benne seeds in the South. The term came from West African slaves who treasured the seed as symbol of luck. Benne seed cookies and wafers are more common in Atlantic coastal cities of South.

¼ cup sesame seeds
½ cup unsalted butter, at room temperature
½ cup sugar, plus more for the glass

1¼ cups all-purpose flour
1½ teaspoons vanilla extract

Preheat the oven to 350°F.

Toast the sesame seeds in a small skillet over low heat for about 4 minutes. Stir the seeds constantly and remove them immediately when they begin to brown. Set them aside.

Cream the butter and sugar on low speed of an electric mixer for about 1 minute. Add the flour to the mixer and mix until incorporated. The dough may look crumbly. Add the vanilla extract and sesame seeds. Mix for about 30 seconds more, or until the seeds are incorporated throughout the dough.

Scoop out the dough with a tablespoon. Place scoops about 1½ inches apart on a light-colored baking sheet. Use your hands to roll each scoop into a ball. Dip the bottom of a drinking glass in sugar. Use the bottom of the glass to gently flatten the dough balls slightly. Dip the bottom of the glass in sugar again before flattening each dough ball.

Bake for 15 minutes. Remove the cookies from the baking sheet to cool.

cooking school

Measure flour onto a sheet of wax or parchment paper. Use the paper to funnel the dry ingredients into the mixer without making a mess.

lazy girl berry cobbler

serves 6 to 8

baking time: 50 minutes

Many Southern grandmothers have a version of this simple cobbler in their recipe boxes. It may just be the quickest way to an old-fashioned farm staple. I first heard it referred to as Lazy Girl Cobbler in Nathalie Dupree's kitchen. Her kitchen is a Southern woman's sanctuary. It's always warm, inviting, and never ceases to be a learning place for the hungry.

½ cup unsalted butter
1 cup Southern All-Purpose Flour (see page 7)
1 cup packed light brown sugar

1 tablespoon baking powder
⅛ teaspoon salt
1¼ cups buttermilk
4 cups fresh blackberries

Preheat the oven to 375°F.

In a 10-inch cast-iron skillet, melt the butter in the oven while it is preheating. Once the butter is melted, remove the skillet from the oven.

Meanwhile, whisk together the flour, brown sugar, baking powder, and salt in a medium mixing bowl. Whisk the buttermilk into the flour mixture.

Pour the batter over the melted butter in the hot skillet. Sprinkle the blackberries evenly over the batter.

Bake for 50 minutes. Serve hot, warm, or at room temperature.

cooking school

Check the bottom of your baking powder can for the expiration date. If it's close to being expired, pour some hot water over a few teaspoons of the questionable powder. If it foams and fizzes immediately, it's still good.

grilled brown sugar peaches

serves 4

Throwing some peaches on the grill is a great way to take advantage of the hot grill after the steaks and burgers are done. (Give the grill rack a quick brushing to avoid picking up flavors from the main course.) Pick peaches that are very ripe; they'll soften up much better as they cook. If you can't smell a peach, it's not ripe.

Vegetable oil
4 large peaches
¼ cup packed light brown sugar
Vanilla ice cream, for serving

Heat the grill to medium (about 350°F).

Dab a paper towel with vegetable oil. Using tongs, wipe the grill rack with the paper towel. The vegetable oil will help prevent the peaches from sticking.

Cut the peaches in half and remove and discard the pits. Lightly brush the cut sides of the peaches with oil. Place the peaches on the grill and grill for 3 minutes per side, or until softened and seared with grill marks.

Meanwhile, place the brown sugar in a medium mixing bowl. Gently toss the hot peaches in the brown sugar and let stand 5 minutes.

Serve the warm peaches and brown sugar sauce over vanilla ice cream.

ambrosia and
white chocolate trifle

serves 8 to 10

Ambrosia was on the table at many a Sunday dinner at Tom's house. She made a simple recipe with just oranges and coconut. I developed this fancy version for a magazine story and this recipe was the cover photograph. It's incredibly beautiful.

1 fresh, cored pineapple, cut into ½-inch
   pieces (about 3½ cups)
8 navel oranges, peeled and cut into
   segments
2 Ruby Red grapefruits, peeled and cut into
   segments

4 ounces white chocolate, chopped
2 cups heavy whipping cream
½ teaspoon vanilla extract
⅛ teaspoon salt

Combine the pineapple, oranges, and grapefruit in a colander set over a mixing bowl. Reserve the juices for another use.

Melt the white chocolate in a mixing bowl set over a saucepan of simmering water. Remove the chocolate from the heat after it melts.

Use an electric mixer to beat the heavy whipping cream until soft peaks form. Add the vanilla extract and salt and beat until stiff peaks form.

Whisk about 1 cup of whipped cream into the melted chocolate. Add the chocolate mixture to the remaining whipped cream and beat just until incorporated, about 10 seconds.

Set aside about ⅓ cup of the fruit mixture. Place half of the fruit in the bottom of a glass trifle dish. Top with half of the white chocolate cream. Repeat the layers. Top with the reserved ⅓ cup of fruit.

cooking school

When choosing a whole pineapple at the store, gently tug on the leaves on top. If a leaf pops out easily, that pineapple is past its prime.

blueberry peach float

serves 4

An underripe and out-of-season peach is tasteless for everyone. If peaches aren't in season, buy frozen peaches. They are peeled, segmented, and then frozen when they are at their best.

3 peaches, peeled
¼ cup peach nectar
¾ cup sparkling water

1 cup fresh blueberries
Vanilla ice cream

Process the peaches and nectar in a food processor fitted with the metal blade. Pour the sparkling water into the food processor and pulse 2 times.

Pour about ⅓ cup of the peach mixture into the bottom of each of 4 glasses. Top with about 2 tablespoons of blueberries and a small scoop of ice cream. Repeat the layers.

Serve immediately.

easy ice cream

makes ½ gallon

As a child, I often tiptoed out the door and dipped my spoon into the massive wooden ice-cream maker that was churning on the back porch. We never waited for it to ripen in the freezer before digging right in. I still prefer ice cream that is soft and creamy in the way that only homemade can be–straight off the churn. If you like a harder, easier-to-scoop ice cream, place it in the freezer for several minutes before serving.

Because this ice cream doesn't have any eggs, it doesn't need to be cooked before freezing. Use the same base to make just about any flavor you desire.

Fruit and extract of choice (see below)
¾ cup milk
¾ cup heavy cream

1 cup sugar
½ cup half-and-half
2 tablespoons freshly squeezed lemon juice

Place the fruit in the bowl of a food processor fitted with the metal blade. Process the fruit until pureed.

Combine the pureed fruit, extract, milk, cream, sugar, half-and-half, and lemon juice in a 4-cup measuring cup.

Set up a half-gallon ice-cream maker according to the manufacturer's instructions. Turn on the machine, then pour the ice-cream mixture into the freezer container. Turning on the machine first keeps any ice cream from sticking to the inside of the freezer container. Freeze according to the manufacturer's instructions.

blueberry
. . . .
1 pint fresh blueberries
¼ teaspoon almond extract

peach
. . . .
3 fresh peaches, peeled
½ teaspoon vanilla extract

strawberry
. . . .
½ pound fresh strawberries, stemmed
½ teaspoon vanilla extract

double chocolate scoop pie

serves 6

I have never turned down a bowl of anything warm and chocolaty topped with ice cream. With both semisweet and dark chocolate in this dreamy dessert, it will be very hard to share. With no crust, it's very easy to serve with a large spoon. Be careful not to overcook the pie. A little gooeyness is good for the soul.

½ cup unsalted butter
¼ cup semisweet chocolate chips
¾ cup sugar
½ cup all-purpose flour
1½ teaspoons vanilla extract

2 large eggs, beaten
1 tablespoon buttermilk
½ cup dark chocolate chips
Vanilla ice cream, for serving

Preheat the oven to 350°F. Lightly grease a 9-inch pie plate.

Melt the butter and semisweet chocolate chips in a medium saucepan over low heat. Remove the saucepan from the heat and whisk in the sugar, flour, and vanilla. While whisking, add the eggs and buttermilk. Fold in the dark chocolate chips. Pour the mixture into the prepared pie plate.

Bake for 16 minutes. The center will not be set. Serve warm with vanilla ice cream.

cooking school

To measure flour and other dry ingredients properly, spoon it into the measuring cup and level it off. Do not pack the flour into the cup. Always use a dry measuring cup for dry ingredients.

real fast pralines.

makes about 30

Pralines call Louisiana home, but different parts of the South say the word differently. "Prah-leen" is said in Cajun country and those of us who live east say "pray-leen." Southerners have enjoyed these famous candies for centuries. My microwave is 1100 watts. Check the wattage of your oven by reading the fine print usually found on the door. If your microwave is stronger than mine, the stirring time will be closer to 5 minutes. If it has less wattage, you'll have the benefit of a shorter stirring time.

¼ cup unsalted butter
1 cup packed light brown sugar
1 cup granulated sugar

1 (5-ounce) can evaporated milk
2 teaspoons vanilla extract
2 cups pecan halves

Lay 2 sheets of wax paper on the countertop. Spray the paper with nonstick cooking spray.

Cut the butter into ½-inch pieces. Combine the sugars in a 2½-quart microwave-safe glass bowl. Stir in the evaporated milk, vanilla, pecan halves, and butter.

Microwave on high for 4½ minutes. Being very careful not to burn yourself, stir well. Microwave for 4 more minutes. Carefully remove from the microwave. Stir while the mixture cools for about 4 to 5 minutes.

You will notice when the mixture begins to thicken slightly and become less shiny. Quickly scoop out with a tablespoon-sized scoop onto the greased wax paper.

(If it has not cooled enough, the pralines will look watery when scooped out.)

Cool completely, about 10 minutes, on wax paper.

upside-down chess pies

serves 6

Chess pie has been around the South since blue and gray were the most popular wardrobe colors. The origins for the name are widely disputed, but the most fun version is that when a cook on a Southern farm was asked what dessert she was cooking, she answered, "Jes pie."

The chocolate wafer on top gives the little pies the crunch of a traditional crust without all the cooking time. Chess pie is traditionally very sweet. My small version is just the right size for this rich confection.

6 chocolate wafer cookies
1¼ cups sugar
1 tablespoon cornmeal
2 tablespoons all-purpose flour
3 eggs

¼ cup milk
1 tablespoon white vinegar
1 teaspoon vanilla extract
¼ cup unsalted butter

Preheat the oven to 375°F.

Lightly spray 6 (4-ounce) ramekins with nonstick cooking spray. Arrange the ramekins on a rimmed baking sheet. Place 1 cookie in the bottom of each ramekin.

Whisk together the sugar, cornmeal, and flour in a medium mixing bowl.

In another medium mixing bowl, whisk together the eggs, milk, vinegar, and vanilla.

Pour the egg mixture into the sugar mixture and whisk until combined. Melt the butter in a microwave and slowly add to the filling. Whisk thoroughly.

Pour the filling into the ramekins. The cookie will float to the top of the filling.

Bake for 22 minutes, or until lightly browned around the edges.

Serve warm or at room temperature.

mini key lime tarts

serves 6

Key lime juice is readily available in the bottled juice section of the grocery store. You can use the bottled version or squeeze lots of the little limes. If you can't get your hands on Key lime juice, use freshly squeezed Persian limes instead.

4 egg yolks
½ cup Key lime juice
1 (14-ounce) can sweetened condensed milk

¼ teaspoon vanilla extract
1 (4-ounce) package mini graham cracker
    piecrusts (6 crusts)

Preheat the oven to 350°F.

Combine the egg yolks, lime juice, sweetened condensed milk, and vanilla together in a medium mixing bowl. Pour the filling into the piecrusts.

Bake for 7 minutes.

cooking school

Key limes are much smaller and more yellow than other limes. They taste sweeter than their larger cousin.

sources

country ham and bacon
Benton's Smoky Mountain Country Hams
www.bentonshams.com
423.442.5003

grits and cornmeal

quick grits
Quaker Oats
www.quakeroats.com

stone-ground grits and cornmeal
Anson Mills
www.ansonmills.com
803.467.4122

flour
White Lily Flour
www.whitelily.com

goat cheese
Sweet Grass Dairy
www.sweetgrassdairy.com
229.228.6704

honey
Savannah Bee Company
www.savannahbee.com
800.955.5080

mayonnaise
Duke's Mayonnaise
www.dukesmayo.com
800.688.5676

pecans and peanuts
Ellis Brothers Pecans
www.werenuts.com
800.635.0616

pecan smoked trout
Woodsmoke Provisions
www.seafoods.com/home.taf
404.355.5125

pepper jelly
Foster's Market
www.fostersmarket.com
919.489.3944

vidalia onions
Vidalia Onion Committee
www.vidaliaonion.org/about_us/buy_
vidalia
912.537.1918

bibliography

A Cook's Tour of Athens. Published by the Junior Assembly of Athens, Georgia. Athens, 1963.

Anderson, Jean. *A Love Affair with Southern Cooking: Recipes and Recollections*. New York: William Morrow, 2007.

Corriher, Shirley O. *BakeWise: The Hows and Whys of Successful Baking with Over 200 Magnificent Recipes*. New York: Scribner, 2008.

Corriher, Shirley O. *CookWise: The Hows and Whys of Successful Cooking with over 230 Great-Tasting Recipes.* New York: William Morrow and Company, Inc., 1997.

Dull, Mrs. S. R. *Southern Cooking*. New York: Grosset and Dunlap, 1941.

Dupree, Nathalie. *New Southern Cooking*. NewYork: Knopf, 1986.

Fowler, Damon Lee. *The Savannah Cookbook*. Layton, UT: GibbsSmith, 2008.

Harris, Joyce Saenz. "Try Some Texas Caviar." *The Dallas Morning News*, August 26, 2009.

Herbst, Sharon Tyler. *The New Food Lover's Companion: Comprehensive Definitions of Nearly 6000 Food, Drink and Culinary Terms*. Third Edition. Hauppauge, NY: Barron's Educational Series, Inc., 2001.

Lobel, David, and Evan Lobel, Mark Lobel, Stanley Lobel. *Lobel's Meat Bible*. San Francisco: Chronicle Books, 2009.

Mariani, John F. *The Dictionary of American Food and Drink.* New York: Hearst, 1997.

Pomo, Jairemarie. *The Hog Island Oyster Lover's Cookbook*. Berkeley: Ten Speed Press, 2007.

The New Encyclopedia of Southern Culture: Volume 7 Foodways. Edited by John T. Edge. Chapel Hill: The University of North Carolina Press, 2007.

Trager, James. *The Food Chronology*. New York: Henry Holt and Company, 1995.

Willis, Virginia. *Bon Appétit, Y'all: Recipes and Stories from Three Generations of Southern Cooking*. Berkeley: Ten Speed Press, 2008.

metric conversions and equivalents

metric conversion formulas

to convert	multiply
Ounces to grams	Ounces by 28.35
Pounds to kilograms	Pounds by .454
Teaspoons to milliliters	Teaspoons by 4.93
Tablespoons to milliliters	Tablespoons by 14.79
Fluid ounces to milliliters	Fluid ounces by 29.57
Cups to milliliters	Cups by 236.59
Cups to liters	Cups by .236
Pints to liters	Pints by .473
Quarts to liters	Quarts by .946
Gallons to liters	Gallons by 3.785
Inches to centimeters	Inches by 2.54

approximate metric equivalents

volume

¼ teaspoon	1 milliliter
½ teaspoon	2.5 milliliters
¾ teaspoon	4 milliliters
1 teaspoon	5 milliliters
1 teaspoon	6 milliliters
1½ teaspoons	7.5 milliliters
1¾ teaspoons	8.5 milliliters
2 teaspoons	10 milliliters
1 tablespoon (½ fluid ounce)	15 milliliters
2 tablespoons (1 fluid ounce)	30 milliliters
¼ cup	60 milliliters
⅓ cup	80 milliliters
½ cup (4 fluid ounces)	120 milliliters
⅔ cup	160 milliliters
¾ cup	180 milliliters
1 cup (8 fluid ounces)	240 milliliters

1¼ cups	300 milliliters
1½ cups (12 fluid ounces)	360 milliliters
1⅔ cups	400 milliliters
2 cups (1 pint)	460 milliliters
3 cups	700 milliliters
4 cups (1 quart)	0.95 liter
1 quart plus ¼ cup	1 liter
4 quarts (1 gallon)	3.8 liters

weight

¼ ounce	7 grams
½ ounce	14 grams
¾ ounce	21 grams
1 ounce	28 grams
1¼ ounces	35 grams
1½ ounces	42.5 grams
1⅔ ounces	45 grams
2 ounces	57 grams
3 ounces	85 grams
4 ounces (¼ pound)	113 grams
5 ounces	142 grams
6 ounces	170 grams
7 ounces	198 grams
8 ounces (½ pound)	227 grams
16 ounces (1 pound)	454 grams
35.25 ounces (2.2 pounds)	1 kilogram

length

⅛ inch	3 millimeters
¼ inch	6 millimeters
½ inch	1¼ centimeters
1 inch	2½ centimeters
2 inches	5 centimeters
2½ inches	6 centimeters
4 inches	10 centimeters
5 inches	13 centimeters
6 inches	15¼ centimeters
12 inches (1 foot)	30 centimeters

oven temperatures

To convert Fahrenheit to Celsius, subtract 32 from Fahrenheit, multiply the result by 5, then divide by 9.

description	fahrenheit	celsius	british gas mark
Very cool	200°	95°	0
Very cool	225°	110°	¼
Very cool	250°	120°	½
Cool	275°	135°	1
Cool	300°	150°	2
Warm	325°	165°	3
Moderate	350°	175°	4
Moderately hot	375°	190°	5
Fairly hot	400°	200°	6
Hot	425°	220°	7
Very hot	450°	230°	8
Very hot	475°	245°	9

common ingredients and their approximate equivalents

1 cup uncooked white rice = 185 grams

1 cup all-purpose flour = 140 grams

1 stick butter (4 ounces • ½ cup • 8 tablespoons) = 110 grams

1 cup butter (8 ounces • 2 sticks • 16 tablespoons) = 220 grams

1 cup brown sugar, firmly packed = 225 grams

1 cup granulated sugar = 200 grams

Information compiled from a variety of sources, including *Recipes into Type* by Joan Whitman and Dolores Simon (Newton, MA: Biscuit Books, 2000); *The New Food Lover's Companion* by Sharon Tyler Herbst (Hauppauge, NY: Barron's, 1995); and *Rosemary Brown's Big Kitchen Instruction Book* (Kansas City, MO: Andrews McMeel, 1998).

index